AF884298

THE JOURNAL JURISPRUDENCE

VOLUME EIGHTEEN

"ENGLISH JURISPRUDENCE"

Contributors: Associate Professor D. Scott Broyles
Charlotte Law School

Professor Allen Shoenberger
Loyola University Chicago School of Law

Dr Guy Lurie
Lately of Georgetown University

Editor: Dr Aron Ping D'Souza
Stawell Chambers, Melbourne

TRINITY TERM
JULY 2013

Elias Clark

PUBLISHED BY THE ELIAS CLARK GROUP
DISTRIBUTED IN CONNECTION WITH THE GALE GROUP,
A PART OF CENGAGE LEARNING

(2013) J. JURIS 67

The Elias Clark Group
www.elias-clark.com

GPO Box 5001
Melbourne, Victoria 3001
Australia

First Published 2013.

Cataloguing-in-Publication entry

Editor: D'Souza, Aron Ping.

Authors: D'Souza, Aron Ping.
Broyles, D. Scott.
Shoenberger, Allen.
Lurie, Guy.

Title: The Journal Jurisprudence, Volume Eighteen.

ISBN: 0980522471 (pbk.)
ISSN: 1836-0955

Subjects: Law – jurisprudence.
Philosophy – general.

This edition may be cited as

(2013) J. Juris.

followed by the page number

ABOUT THE TYPEFACE

The Journal Jurisprudence is typeset in Garamond 12 and the footnotes are set in Garamond 10. The typeface was named for Claude Garamond (c. 1480 - 1561) and are based on the work of Jean Jannon. By 1540, Garamond became a popular choice in the books of the French imperial court, particularly under King Francis I. Garamond was said to be based on the handwriting of Angelo Vergecio, a librarian to the King. The italics of Garamond are credited to Robert Grandjon, an assistant to Claude Garamond. The font was re-popularised in the art deco era and became a mainstay on twentieth-century publication. In the 1970s, the font was redesigned by the International Typeface Corporation, which forms the basis of the variant of Garamond used in this Journal.

TABLE OF CONTENTS

CALL FOR PAPERS

The field of jurisprudence lies at the nexus of law and politics, the practical and the philosophical. By understanding the theoretical foundations of law, jurisprudence can inform us of the place of legal structures within larger philosophical frameworks. In its inaugural edition, *The Journal Jurisprudence* received many creative and telling answers to the question, "What is Law?" For the second edition, the editors challenged the scholarly and lay communities to inquire into intersection between jurisprudence and economics.

With the backing of our diverse and disparate community, *The Journal Jurisprudence* has now evolved into a distinct format. We will no longer be setting a question for each issue, but instead designing issues around the articles we received. Therefore, we invite scholars, lawyers, judges, philosophers and lay people to tackle any and all of the great questions of law. Knowing that ideas come in all forms, papers can be of any length, although emphasis is placed on readability by lay audiences.

Papers may engage with case studies, intellectual arguments or any other method that answers philosophical questions applicable to the law. Importantly, articles will be selected based upon quality and the readability of works by non-specialists. The intent of the Journal is to involve non-scholars in the important debates of legal philosophy.

The Journal also welcomes and encourages submissions of articles typically not found in law journals, including opinionated or personalised insights into the philosophy of law and its applications to practical situations.

Jurisprudence is published four times per year, to coincide with the four terms of the legal year, in an attractive paperback and electronic edition.

Each author who submits to this volume will be provided with a complimentary copy of the journal.

Length:	Any length is acceptable, although readability to non-specialist is key.
Presentation Style:	Papers must comply with the Australian Guide to Legal Citations, Second Edition published by the Melbourne University Law Review. An electronic edition is available at, http://mulr.law.unimelb.edu.au/PDFs/aglc_dl.pdf
Submission:	You must submit electronically in Microsoft Word format to editor@jurisprudence.com.au. Extraneous formatting is discouraged.

Correspondence can also be sent to this address. If you are considering submitting an article, you are invited to contact the editor to discuss ideas before authoring a work.

SUBSCRIPTION INFORMATION

The Journal is published four times per year in an attractive softcover book. Subscription to the Journal can be achieved by two methods:

1) Single issues can be purchased on amazon.com. Our publishers, the Elias Clark Group, set a retail price for each edition, typically AU$40. However, due to their agreement with amazon.com, the price may vary for retail customers.

2) A subscription to the Journal can be purchased for AU$150 per year, or AU$280 for two years. This price includes postage throughout the world. Payment can be made by international bank cheque, but not a personal cheque, to:

The Journal Jurisprudence,
C/o The Elias Clark Group
GPO Box 5001
Melbourne, Victoria, Australia.

Alternatively, the Journal is available online at www.jurisprudence.com.au and can be read there free of charge.

SHAKESPEARE'S REFLECTIONS ON LOVE AND LAW IN ROMEO AND JULIET

D. SCOTT BROYLES*

ABSTRACT: This Article examines Shakespeare's teaching in *Romeo & Juliet* about the power of love and the role of law. Broadly speaking, the play is about how the tragic death of the two young lovers overcomes the hatred between their families. At a deeper level, the play invites the reader to reflect upon the proper relationship between religion, and the political community and its laws, between divine love and human love. In the end, Romeo and Juliet points not only to the superiority of the proper separation of church and state, but also toward the possibility of an honorable faith that can exist alongside and support a vibrant political community—a possible reconciliation between love and law.

"Never was there a story of more woe," the Prince of Verona tells us at play's end, "than this of Juliet and her Romeo."[1] Shakespeare's tragic play, Romeo and Juliet, moves the reader through its hauntingly beautiful depiction of the "misadventured piteous overthrows" of the "star-crossed lovers."[2] Yet, that is not the whole story, for Shakespeare places the love of Romeo and Juliet within the context of a larger plot: Friar Laurence's (misguided) effort to restore political harmony in Verona by grounding the rule of law on a new foundation: a foundation of Christian love and contrition. The love-theme of Romeo and Juliet, then, is to be understood within this larger political theme as Shakespeare presents it to us in the Prologue:

* Associate Professor of Law, Charlotte School of Law, J.D. Washington & Lee School of Law, PhD Institute of Philosophic Studies, University of Dallas. I am much indebted to the thoughtful input of Professors John Alvis and Thomas G. West, as well as my research assistants Jennifer Blair-Smith and Carly Blades

[1] WILLIAM SHAKESPEARE, Romeo and Juliet, in WILLIAM SHAKESPEARE: THE COMPLETE WORKS 5.3.329-30 (Alfred Harbage ed., The Viking Press 1977) (1595) (The quotations from Shakespeare offered here are those of the Pelican edition).
[2] *Id.* at Prologue, 6-7.

Two households, both alike in dignity,
In fair Verona, where we lay our scene,
From ancient grudge break to new mutiny,
Where civil blood makes civil hands unclean.
From forth the fatal loins of these two foes
A pair of star-cross'd lovers take their life;
Whose mis-adventured piteous overthrows
Doth with their death bury their parents' strife.[3]

Broadly speaking, the play is about how the tragic death of the two young lovers overcomes the hatred between their families. At a deeper level, the play invites the reader to reflect upon the proper relationship between Christianity and the political community and its laws, between divine love and human love. In the final analysis, Romeo and Juliet represents a fruitful picture of how the Church of Rome's mistreatment of Christianity leads to political decline, while hinting at the possibility of a healthy Christian political community.

The sad state of Catholic Verona, like Catholic Italy itself, constitutes a grave political problem. The Catholic Church's distorted understanding of the relationship between Christianity and politics actually helps create the political problem it later seeks to solve through its agent, Friar Laurence. The Church does this first through its assumption of political power and then through its efforts to reformulate the traditional understanding of justice. This effort at reformulation is carried forward by Friar Laurence, as he initially seeks to establish love and mercy as the foundation of law and justice. Two principal problems emerge from this effort as the play progresses, and these problems can be stated as lessons to be drawn from the play: (1) political and legal decisions based on the principles of love (and loving acts of mercy) are incapable of restraining the more violent and destructive human passions, such as greed, avarice, envy, and unprincipled ambition, and (2) when the transpolitical form of Christian love depicted in the play comes to supplant the traditional understanding of law and justice, civic life is robbed of its proper vitality. The competitiveness of citizens contending for public recognition by virtue of their respective claims to excellence is undermined. In short, the assumption of power by popes and priests in the name of supernatural authority and doctrines, as well as the

[3] *Id.* at 1–8.

imposition of those doctrines on matters political, has left Verona a lawless place "[w]here civil blood makes civil hands unclean."

With civic virtue and respect for the rule of law undermined in Verona, the political scene has deteriorated into tribal factionalism. The efforts by the Prince and Friar Laurence to correct the city's factionalism through a misguided resort to Christian love and mercy only lead to greater bloodshed in general and an uncertain peace. Indeed, the bloody results of these efforts lead a desperate Friar Laurence to employ other spiritual stratagems—specifically consciousness of sin and the resulting guilt—in the hope of salvaging the disintegrating situation.

As the standard of brotherly love supplants honorific competitiveness, the political life retains little attraction for those spirited souls, such as Romeo, who yearn for lives that experience the heights of human potential. As a result, Romeo's erotic soul attaches itself to the only remaining object of worth: the beautiful, as it manifests itself first in Rosaline, and ultimately in Juliet. Such beauty offers Romeo not only an unsullied object of his desire, but an escape from a world that otherwise holds little attraction for him. In the end, such all-consuming desire for the beautiful careens out of control, and leads to violence and ultimately, to death.

But it is also the case that, for Romeo and Juliet, the character of their love is powerfully influenced by particular, albeit different, Christian understandings of love. Romeo's understanding of love is connected to his general contempt of this world and transforms his erotic attachment to Juliet into a private religion that is doomed ("death-marked") from the start.

As will be argued, this transformation of Eros[4] into a religion of love is a tendency to which erotic love is naturally prone. This natural tendency is exacerbated by that Christian teaching—perhaps a distorted Christian teaching—which exalts heavenly things to such an extent that worldly concerns are unduly diminished. Through his depiction of Juliet's perception of love, however, Shakespeare seems to offer a sounder alternative understanding of the proper balance between human and divine love. In the end, Romeo and Juliet is a tragedy, but none of the characters seems to embody the kind of virtue one might properly consider heroic in nature. The play's tragic nature may be best understood in the heroic but doomed efforts of Romeo and Friar Laurence—each in his own way—to

[4] "Eros" will be capitalized throughout this essay in a manner consistent with the depiction of Eros as the god of love.

reconcile or transcend the tension between the merely human and the political, on the one hand, and divine love on the other.

Few critics, however, have found this play about love to convey a significant political teaching. As one writer has noted, these critics find the central themes to

> rang[e] from a literal insistence on the lovers' star-crossed fate, to a Freudian view of their experience as an embodiment of the death-wish; from a neo-orthodox-Elizabethan lesson in the dangers of passion, to a providential triumph of love over hate.[5]

Three notable exceptions to these non-political critics can be found in essays by Allan Bloom, David M. Wagner, and Jerry Weinberger. All three provide helpful insights into the political philosophy of Romeo and Juliet.[6]

Bloom argues that the play reveals the "natural rights" of love and how the necessities and demands of the "anti-erotic" family are in tension with those natural rights.[7] While his essay develops the theme of love and friendship, Bloom also points to the corrupting effect Christian mercy has on the political and shows how Italy at the time suffered the effects of that corruption.[8] Wagner takes issue with Bloom's argument regarding the family, contending that the play reveals the need to re-found the family. A re-founding in which Romeo and Juliet reject the patriarchal ordering of the family as a means to advance their social and economic position and replace it with the kind of genuine love that can be the "seedbed of love and civic virtue."[9]

Weinberger's essay is perhaps the best analysis of the play to date. Expanding on some of Bloom's observations, Weinberger's thesis is that Shakespeare wrote Romeo and Juliet in large part to present his readers with an "especially fruitful picture" of the problem Christianity posed to the Western political world—a problem which led to the attempted solution

---

[5] Douglas Cole, *Introduction*, *in* TWENTIETH CENTURY INTERPRETATIONS OF ROMEO AND JULIET 12 (Douglas Cole. ed., 1970).

[6] ALLAN BLOOM, LOVE AND FRIENDSHIP (1993); David M. Wagner, Civil Blood, THE CLAREMONT INSTITUTE, Sept. 17, 2002, http://www.claremont.org; Jerry Weinberger, Pious Princes and Red-Hot Lovers: The Politics of Shakespeare's *Romeo and Juliet*, 65 J. POL. 350-75 (2003).

[7] BLOOM, *supra* note 6, at 276.

[8] BLOOM, *supra* note 6, at 292-96.

[9] WAGNER, *supra* note 6, at 10.

(via Machiavelli) that is modern politics.[10] The play's tragic outcome, Weinberger contends, is an indictment of Christianity's baleful effect upon political life:

> All this is due to the softness of the pious Prince, who believes along with the friar that heaven has been at work, the soft quarreling of a christianized and softened aristocracy, and the political meddling of a friar, whose morality sides with the people in two crucial respects: he sees all men as equal in the eyes of God and in their contamination by original sin, and he aims, in effect, fanatically at what the people most want: peace. Neither the Prince nor the friar intended this political outcome of the play. But it is the clear secular effect of their Christian motives.[11]

Weinberger's argument that Machiavelli was critical of what he believed to be Christianity's corrosive effect on political life is compelling. Moreover, it is consistent with what Leo Strauss, a noted scholar of Machiavelli, has maintained:

> He [Machiavelli] goes on to explain why, or by virtue of what, Christianity has led the world into weakness. By showing the truth and the true way, Christianity has lowered the esteem for 'the honor of the world,' whereas the pagans regarded that honor as the highest good and were therefore more ferocious or less weak in their actions.[12]

According to Bloom, Weinberger and Strauss, Machiavelli believes the honors bestowed on those who serve the common good, and that motivate such public servants, are jeopardized by the Christian depreciation of worldly goods in the name of humility and in favor of heavenly rewards. But to suggest that Machiavelli held this view of Christianity does not establish that Shakespeare did so as well.

The argument of this essay is that Bloom, Wagner, and Weinberger are correct, but only partially so. Instead of an attack on Christianity *per se*, Romeo and Juliet represents a fruitful picture of how the Church of Rome's mistreatment of Christianity leads to political decline. Moreover,

---

[10] WEINBERGER, *supra* note 6, at 352.
[11] WEINBERGER, *supra* note 6, at 370.
[12] LEO STRAUSS, THOUGHTS OF MACHIAVELLI,178(1958).

Shakespeare leads his attentive readers to recognize not only the bad example of Friar Laurence's Catholicism—including its deleterious effects on erotic love—but also a healthier alternative understanding of Christianity in the dedication to holy marriage as seen through Juliet's thoughts and decisions. The combination of these two understandings does point toward modernity in the form of the separation of church and state. It is a modern state, however, that seeks to retain Christianity's excellences, while restricting its jurisdiction over matters beyond its proper mandate.

The City and Its Laws

All is not well in "fair Verona," with the "civil hands" of two feuding families producing the continuing shedding of "civil blood." The ostensible cause of the factional warfare, it would seem, is unimportant: it is "born of an airy word / By thee, old Capulet, and Montague . . . ."[13] No profound injustice on either house's part began the fray. Rather, they fight for insignificant reasons. The forces tending to faction are more powerful than any forces tending to unite. James Madison could well have had this play in mind when he wrote about factions in Federalist 10:

> So strong is this propensity of mankind to fall into mutual animosities, that where no substantial occasion presents itself, the most frivolous and fanciful distinctions have been sufficient to kindle their unfriendly passions and excite their most violent conflicts.[14]

Understanding the deeper cause of the illness afflicting the city's soul requires further consideration.

The attitudes of Verona's citizens toward the city's laws provide a helpful starting point for reflection. The particular laws of a city or political community reflect, to greater and lesser degrees, the more comprehensive understanding of the political community's good as a whole.[15] This

---

[13] SHAKESPEARE, *supra* note 1, at 1.1.83.

[14] THE FEDERALIST 10, at 79 (James Madison) (The New American library, Inc: New York, New York, 1962).

[15] ARISTOTLE, ARISTOTLE'S POLITICS, 1280b 10 (W.D. Ross ed., Oxford UP 1957): "Since we see that every polis is a community, and that every community is established for the sake of some good—since all do everything for the sake of what seems to them good—it is clear that all communities aim at some good, the one that does so in the highest degree and

comprehensive understanding of the good of the political community as reflected in its laws is also known as its understanding of justice: "The laws make pronouncements on every sphere of life, and their aim is to secure either the common good of all or of the best . . . accordingly, in one sense we call those things 'just' which produce and preserve happiness for the social and political community."[16] The honors and material goods are distributed according to the dictates of justice, and justice is understood within the context of the good—or ends—aimed at by the political community.[17] This distribution mandates that equals are treated equally, and unequals are treated unequally.[18] These traditional principles of law and justice set forth in books such as the writings of Aristotle and The Federalist reveal the potential excellence associated with the noblest aspects of political activity.

Given the sorry state of Verona's political landscape, one should not be surprised to find that the eleven references to "the law" throughout the play are mocking or deprecating. None is respectful or deferential to the dignity or higher purposes of the rule of law. The play opens on such a note. The brawlers in the opening scene, Sampson and Gregory, servants of the house of Capulet, seek to manipulate the law in order to gain an advantage: "Is the law of our side, if I say ay?"[19] Mercutio speaks of lawyers as mere money-grubbers in his rambling discourse on Queen Mab: "O'er lawyers' fingers, who straight dream on fees...."[20] Justice receives but one reference in the play, and it is ultimately dismissed in the name of mercy.

As will be discussed below, of greater significance are Romeo's and Friar Laurence's denigrations of the rule of law and the proper understanding of justice. Of the play's eleven references to the law, four are Friar Laurence's. In his effort to console Romeo regarding his banishment, Friar Laurence praises the Prince's (now second) act of "mercy," contrasting it favorably with the city's stern law of death. In the midst of a discussion that occurs at the very center of the play, Friar Laurence commends the "kind" Prince for

aims at the most authoritative of all goods is the community which is the most authoritative of all and embraces all others: this is the one called the polis or the political community."

16 ARISTOTLE, ARISTOTLE'S ETHICS, 1129B 13-18 (Martin Ostwald, ed., the Liberal Arts Press, Inc. a Division of the Bobbs-Merrill Co., Inc.: Indianapolis, Ind., 1962). See also THE FEDERALIST 51, at 324 (James Madison): "Justice is the end of government. It is the end of civil society. It ever has been and ever will be pursued until it be obtained, or until liberty be lost in the pursuit."

17 ARISTOTLE, *supra* note 16, at 1281a 1-15.

18 ARISTOTLE, *supra* note 16, at 1281a 1-15.

19 SHAKESPEARE, *supra* note 1, at 1.1.45.

20 SHAKESPEARE, *supra* note 1, at 1.4.73.

having "rush'd aside the law," choosing mercy instead.[21] For Friar Laurence, it is only when the higher law of Christian mercy transforms, or even supplants, the human law that it truly serves justice. Romeo, too, depreciates the law in that it cannot aid the poor. He encourages the apothecary to break the law to escape his poverty: "The world is not thy friend nor the world's law / The world affords no law to make thee rich / Then be not poor, but break it, and take this."[22] In contrast to Friar Laurence's (and Romeo's) understanding of justice, is that of bloody Verona. The play's single reference to "justice" is Lady Capulet's demand for Romeo's execution after he has slain Tybalt.[23] The city's laws diminish when they compete with the higher law of Christian mercy. In Verona, then, we find a city beset by factional fighting and a low regard for the rule of law. But what, if anything, does Verona's relationship to Italy as a whole reveal?

While there are numerous references to Verona in Romeo and Juliet,[24] there is but a single reference (by cynical Mercutio) to Italy.[25] Nor do we find in Romeo and Juliet the manifest concern with the fate of the Roman nation that occupies the thoughts of the major characters in Shakespeare's Roman plays, such as Coriolanus and Julius Caesar, or his narrative poem, The Rape of Lucrece. Not only is there a discernible lack of national pride in Romeo and Juliet, the Italian city into which the lovers are born is likewise far removed from the timocratic state Shakespeare depicts in his Roman works, where honor in the sense of public acclaim moves the souls of the noble citizens. As Professor John Alvis has observed, Shakespeare's works concerning Rome are noted for their extensive treatment of honor:

> Roman history provides matter for four plays and a lengthy narrative poem.[26] These works feature plots that in every instance turn upon issues of honor: The violation of a woman's honor, a soldier's quest for recognition, a statesman's decision to uphold his reputation for

[21] SHAKESPEARE, *supra* note 1, at 3.3.25–26.
[22] SHAKESPEARE, *supra* note 1, at 5.1.72–74.
[23] SHAKESPEARE, *supra* note 1, at 3.1.189–90.
[24] SHAKESPEARE, *supra* note 1, at Prologue, 2; 1.1.90; 1.2.35; 1.2.86; 1.3.77; 1.5.67; 3.1.87; 3.3.15; 5.1.12; 5.3.300.
[25] SHAKESPEARE, *supra* note 1, at 3.1.2.
[26] The author is referring to Titus Andronicus, Coriolanus, Julius Caesar, Antony and Cleopatra, and The Rape of Lucrece.

patriotism by slaying a despot, a lover's attempt to combine hedonism with personal fidelity for the sake of glory.[27]

Alvis' observation is amply supported in the text of Shakespeare's Roman works. Coriolanus refuses to flatter the commoners, because they are dishonorable in his eyes, even though refusing to do so will ultimately cost him his life:

I will not do't
Lest I surcease to honour my own truth,
And by my body's action teach my mind
A most inherent baseness.[28]

In Julius Caesar, Brutus pronounces his dedication to the common good of Rome in terms of his honor:

Set honor in one eye and death i' th' other,
And I will look on both indifferently;
For let the gods so speed as I love
The name of honor more than I fear death.[29]

In the wake of her rape, Lucrece turns to suicide in order to reclaim her honor:

My honor I'll bequeath unto the knife
That wounds my body so dishonored.
'Tis honor to deprive dishonored life:
The one will live the other being dead.
So of shame's ashes shall my fame be bred,
For in my death I murder shameful scorn;
My shame so dead, mine honor is new born.[30]

It is the spirited, honorific souls, Aristotle tells us, who tend to shape the spirit of the city itself.[31] It is worth noting, then, that Romeo and Juliet

---

[27] JOHN ALVIS, SHAKESPEARE'S UNDERSTANDING OF HONOR 12 (Carolina Academic Press 1990). Alvis' book provides an excellent study of Shakespeare's thematic teaching on honor.

[28] WILLIAM SHAKESPEARE, Coriolanus, in WILLIAM SHAKESPEARE: THE COMPLETE WORKS 3.3.120-123 (Alfred Harbage ed., The Viking Press 1977) (1595).

[29] WILLIAM SHAKESPEARE, Julius Caesar, in WILLIAM SHAKESPEARE: THE COMPLETE WORKS 1.2.86-89 (Alfred Harbage ed., The Viking Press 1977) (1595).

[30] WILLIAM SHAKESPEARE, The Rape of Lucrece, in WILLIAM SHAKESPEARE: THE COMPLETE WORKS 1184-90 (Alfred Harbage ed., The Viking Press 1977) (1595).

[31] ARISTOTLE, *supra* note 16, at 1095b.

contains few references to "honor."[32] One finds no expressions of public honor or spiritedness by the players in Romeo and Juliet that could be considered similar to the Roman works. The sole exception, as will be discussed at the conclusion of this essay, is that of Juliet, who connects her marital fidelity with honor and her faith. But even Juliet lacks the sense of honor that is peculiarly public or patriotic in character.

This latter Rome, on display in Verona, is bereft of the honor-seeking citizens of pre-Christian Rome. By far the most interesting thing Verona can produce is the personal love story of the "death-marked lovers." While Verona may be "fair," it is not timocratic. Neither house justifies its fighting the other on the grounds of superior merit. Love, as it manifests itself in the personal and the political, is the key to the play. While Romeo and Juliet are at its center, neither ultimately determines the play's action, at least they do not do so in any self-conscious sense. To a considerable extent, they appear subject to forces beyond their control whether operating from within their own souls or on their souls from without.

With the notable exceptions of Friar Laurence and the Prince, the play's characters are either apolitical or political merely in the sense of supporting one or the other of the warring factions. Largely, the characters are either lovers or quarrelers. Even the Prince, the play's principle political figure, indulges in mainly empty threats of punishment—appealing to "peace" and the tradition of the families.[33] He does not speak to the citizens of Verona as "Italians" or "Citizens of Proud Verona." Romeo, when we first meet him, is disgusted by the political situation: "What fray was here? Yet tell me not, for I have heard it all."[34] Tybalt scorns the communal order, that "peace" to which the Prince appeals: "I hate the word / As I hate hell . . . ."[35] Opposed to Tybalt are the citizens, who appear concerned with nothing other than maintaining the peace.[36] The Church's agent, Friar Laurence, is more effectual than the Prince, and he will deliver the citizens their peace through his machinations. But Friar Laurence's peace will likely be short-lived: in the end, it will be a "glooming peace."[37]

---

[32] Tybalt more closely resembles the honorific soul than does any other character in the play. However "fiery" Tybalt's understanding of honor is purely reflexive and angry, containing no reflection or awareness of honor's higher aspects, and rooted only in familial allegiance, the "stock and honor of my kin." SHAKESPEARE, *supra* note 1, at 1.5.58.
[33] SHAKESPEARE, *supra* note 1, at 1.1.79.
[34] SHAKESPEARE, *supra* note 1, at 1.1.172.
[35] SHAKESPEARE, *supra* note 1, at 1.1.67–68.
[36] SHAKESPEARE, *supra* note 1, at 1.1.72 -73; 3.1.136 37, 39 – 40.00
[37] SHAKESPEARE, *supra* note 1, at 5.3.5.

There simply is no larger sense of civic purpose, public honor, patriotism, or justice in the play. The factions fight, and the city suffers. This political aimlessness is reflected in the sense of contrariness and apparent accident that characterizes the manner in which the events of the play unfold: from Romeo's rambling discourse on the clashing and paradoxical nature of love,[38] to Friar John's failure to get the news of Juliet to Romeo because of the plague,[39] or Romeo's suicide occurring just before Juliet awakens.[40] How do the play's characters help us understand this enfeebled state of affairs in which Verona (and Italy) finds itself?

The Prince: The Political Response

In The Discourses, Machiavelli treats, at some length, the problem of Italy's politically divided cities, identifying Italy's Roman Catholicism as the ultimate source of the political trouble.[41] Shakespeare clearly presents Verona as one such city, rendered weak by factional discord. Machiavelli sets forth the manner in which a divided city must be united with stark clarity:

> For it is necessary to pick one of three modes: either to kill them, as they did; or to remove them from the city; or to make them make peace together under obligations not to offend one another. Of these three modes, this last is most harmful, least certain, and most useless... But without doubt the first [mode] would have been most secure. Because such executions have in them something of the great and of the generous, however, a weak republic does not know how to do them and is so distant from them that it is led to the second remedy only with trouble. These are among the errors I told of at the beginning that the princes of our times make who have to judge great things, for they ought to wish to hear how those who have had to judge such cases in antiquity governed themselves. But the weakness of men

[38] SHAKESPEARE, *supra* note 1, at 1.1.169 -180.
[39] SHAKESPEARE, *supra* note 1, at 5.2.14 -16.
[40] SHAKESPEARE, *supra* note 1, at 5.3.119 – 147.
[41] NICCOLO MACHIAVELLI, THE DISCOURSES ON LIVY 37-38 (Harvey C. Mansfield & Nathan Tarkov trans., University of Chicago Press 1996).

> at present, caused by their weak education and their slight knowledge of things, makes them judge ancient judgments in part inhuman, in part impossible.[42]

Prince Escalus seems to have been taken straight from Machiavelli's model of the weak ruler. The citizens do not readily listen to him: "Will they not hear? What, ho! you men, you

beasts . . . ."[43] He initially embraces Machiavelli's "most hurtful, the least reliable and the most futile" method after he confronts the initial letting of "civil blood." However, as the Prince tells us, this is the third such "civil brawl." After he solemnly declares that death will be the sentence "if ever you disturb our streets again . . . ," he does not follow through.[44] After the ensuing (fourth) brawl, the Prince exiles Romeo for killing Tybalt rather than sentencing him to death.[45]

Banishing Romeo is Machiavelli's second remedy, which characterizes a weak republic. Since the law dictates Romeo's death, the Prince effectively ignores his own counsel: "Mercy but murders, pardoning those that kill."[46] As Machiavelli predicts, the Prince mercifully spares Romeo the "inhuman" punishment the law decrees.

The Prince's second failure to apply the law, choosing mercy instead, contributes to another unnecessary death—that of County Paris at Romeo's hands. The Prince's disposition to choose mercy over the commands of the law, even while being conscious of the problematic nature of his choice, reveals the Catholic Church's influence on his political judgment. It reveals, in Machiavelli's words, his "defective education." Even his final pronouncement reveals this influence: "See what a scourge is laid upon your hate / That heaven finds means to kill your joys with love."[47] The Prince is deferential to the representative of Rome, Friar Laurence. When it becomes clear at the play's end how entangled the friar is in the events leading to the deaths of Romeo, Juliet, and Paris, the Prince refuses to punish or even criticize him: "[w]e still have known thee for a holy man" is all the Prince says.[48] In effect, the Prince says, "because you are the holy representative of

---

42 MACHIAVELLI, *supra* note 41, at 274-75.
43 SHAKESPEARE, *supra* note 1, at 1.1.77.
44 SHAKESPEARE, *supra* note 1, at 1.1.90.
45 SHAKESPEARE, *supra* note 1, at 3.1.184-95.
46 SHAKESPEARE, *supra* note 1, at 3.1.195.
47 SHAKESPEARE, *supra* note 1, at 5.3.292–93.
48 SHAKESPEARE, *supra* note 1, at 5.3.269.

Rome, you must be given every presumption of innocence." The Prince's submission to the Church's authority is apparent.

As noted earlier, when addressing the citizens, the Prince never refers to "Italy" or "Italians." The play's only reference to "Italy"[49] is made by the cynical Mercutio, who alone seems concerned with maintaining national pride and is critical of the "French" influence on Italian customs.[50] While there is but the single reference to "Italy" in the play, there are three references to "Saint Peter's Church," indicating the latter's greater influence.[51] The Church's representative is Friar Laurence.

Friar Laurence: Ecclesiastical Politics and The Regime of Prefect Love

Concerning the Catholic Church's role in the Italian cities' decline, Machiavelli wrote as follows:

> The cause that Italy is not in the same condition [united] and does not also have one republic or one prince to govern it is solely the church… Thus, since the church has not been powerful enough to be able to seize Italy, nor permitted another to seize it, it has been the cause that [Italy] has not been able to come under one head but has been under many princes and lords, from whom so much disunion and so much weakness have arisen that it has been led to be the prey not only of barbarian powers but of whoever assaults it. For this we other Italians have an obligation to the church and not to others.[52]

Prior to Machiavelli, Dante expressed similar concerns regarding the Church of Rome in The Divine Comedy. In Canto 16 of Purgatory, Dante approves Marco Lombardo's claim that

> Rome, which made the world good, was wont to have Two Suns, which made visible both the one road and the other, that of the world and that of god. The one

[49] SHAKESPEARE, *supra* note 1, at 3.1.2.
[50] SHAKESPEARE, *supra* note 1, at 2.2.43.
[51] SHAKESPEARE, *supra* note 1, at 3.5.115, 117, 155.
[52] MACHIAVELLI, *supra* note 41, at 1:12.

> has quenched the other, and the sword is joined to the crook: and the one together with the other must perforce go ill.... the Church of Rome, by confounding in itself two governments, falls in the mire and befouls both itself and its burden.[53]

Dante bemoans the state of 14th century Italy: "Ah, Italy enslaved, hostel of misery, ship without pilot in great tempest, no princess among the provinces but a brothel!"[54] Factionalism is rampant throughout the country: "For all the cities of Italy are full of tyrants and every clown that plays the partisan becomes a Marcellus."[55] Two of the warring families Dante specifically identifies in Canto 6 are the "Montagues and Capulets."[56] The problem facing Italy, Dante suggests, is twofold: the absence of the Holy Roman Emperor and the pernicious influence of ecclesiastical politics.

Shakespeare's play presents the state of Italian politics in a manner notably similar to the descriptions provided by Machiavelli and Dante. Dante criticizes those priests who seek to usurp the civil authority in the name of the Roman church: "Ah, ye that should be devout and let Caesar sit in the saddle if you gave good heed to God's direction to you, see how this beast has turned vicious for lack of correction by the spurs since you laid hold of the bridle."[57] Shakespeare depicts Friar Laurence in a similar fashion. As the dutiful agent of the Church of Rome, Friar Laurence lays hold of the bridle and controls the action of the play more directly than any other character. The results are disastrous.

When we first meet the Franciscan Friar Laurence, it is early in the morning. Surprisingly, the friar is not at prayer but, instead, is filling up his wicker basket with "baleful weeds and precious-juiced flowers."[58] In fact, we never encounter Friar Laurence, or any character in the play, at prayer. As he goes about his business, the friar meditates on the nature of man and how man's nature reflects the innate qualities to be found in nature herself. Indeed, the friar appears to be a serious student of nature, and we see that the potion he

---

53 Dante Aligheri, The Divine Comedy of Dante Alighieri: Purgatorio Canto XVI at 106 – 12, 127-29 (John D. Sinclair ed., Oxford UP 1979).

54 *Id.* at 78–80.

55 *Id.* at 123.

56 *Id.* at 106. Given Shakespeare's choice of the Montagues and Capulets as the representative families of his play, and Dante's use of the same names, along with similar depictions of the political and religious situation plaguing Verona, it would seem to be a reasonable assumption that Shakespeare intended the time period of Romeo and Juliet to be the 14th century.

57 *Id.* at 6.91–95.

58 SHAKESPEARE, *supra* note 1, at 3.3.8.

will later give to Juliet is likely the result of his studies: "Within the infant rind of this weak flower / Poison hath residence, and medicine power / For this, being smelt, with that part cheers each part / Being tasted, slays all senses with the heart."[59]

While the friar speaks about grace, it is of the natural rather than supernatural variety.[60] Moreover, his comments about human nature are surprisingly political and are not what one might consider a more orthodox Christian understanding: "Virtue itself turns vice, being misapplied / And vice sometime's by action dignified."[61] It is a curious form of Christian doctrine that holds a successful outcome can dignify vice. Necessity may justify vice, but orthodox Christian teaching would not hold that it dignifies it. The friar seems less concerned with the spiritual aspects of his calling than he is with practical considerations—medicine and the political consequences of moral decisions—that he later refers to as "my art."[62] In his private reveries, we see a friar whose reflections on the practical aspects of life are consistent with one who is ready to lay hold of the city's "bridle." Indeed, the friar will soon put his thoughts into action. It is in the midst of these reveries that Romeo approaches Friar Laurence asking him to perform the marriage ceremony. In agreeing to do so, Friar Laurence believes he is dignifying the vice of an ill-advised marriage by acting for the greater good of a peaceful Verona. What the friar does not know is that he is actually turning virtue into vice by misapplying Christian love in his effort to rid Verona of its civic strife.

Friar Laurence is not obtuse, and he knows Romeo's passion for Juliet is far short of anything resembling a mature, authentic love. He chides Romeo for having abandoned his "love" for Rosaline at the first sight of Juliet: "Young men's love then lies / Not truly in their hearts, but in their eyes."[63] The friar instructs his student on the difference between youthful longing and true love, criticizing Romeo for "doting, not for loving, pupil mine."[64] Nevertheless, he agrees to marry Romeo and Juliet: "For this alliance may so happy prove / To turn your households' rancor to pure love."[65] At first blush, the friar's goal seems laudable, but upon further reflection, it is remarkably presumptuous. The friar will marry Romeo and Juliet, not

---

[59] SHAKESPEARE, *supra* note 1, at 2.3.23–26.
[60] SHAKESPEARE, *supra* note 1, at 2.3.14, 28.
[61] SHAKESPEARE, *supra* note 1, at 2.3.21–22.
[62] SHAKESPEARE, *supra* note 1, at 5.3.243.
[63] SHAKESPEARE, *supra* note 1, at 2.3.67–68.
[64] SHAKESPEARE, *supra* note 1, at 2.3.82.
[65] SHAKESPEARE, *supra* note 1, at 2.3.91–92.

because it is wise for them to be married—their love is suspect at best—but because he will thereby transform the civic life of Verona itself, creating "pure love" where factionalism once reigned. Friar Laurence's agenda is to resolve the city's factional problem through the marriage. This is far beyond the more reasonable and modest expectation of tempering factional discord. Friar Laurence wants his new society to be one that lives and is ruled by love, not harsh justice. He opposes the universalism of Christian love to the families' political factionalism so that common brotherhood will come to dominate over political distinctions. Rather than respect and fear the rule of law, the friar will bring the Capulets and Montagues to love one another.

It is important to note that Shakespeare himself tells us at the beginning of the play that a scheme such as the friar's marriage plan will not work to quench "the continuance of their parents' rage / Which, but their children's end, naught could remove."[66] Confirming what he indicated in the Prologue, Shakespeare reveals that even if the friar had succeeded in marrying Romeo and Juliet, their parents' rage would not have been quenched, and the young lovers would probably have had to live in exile in order to stay married. Such rebelliousness by their children would not likely have been tolerated by the parents, and we certainly see this play out later in their furious reaction to Juliet's refusal to marry Paris.[67]

Friar Laurence's plan is flawed, and his competence in such political matters falls short. He lacks prudence. The friar is incapable of salvaging the flawed marriage plan when it goes awry by the imminent marriage of Juliet and Paris. It was no secret that the Capulets were interested in Juliet marrying Paris.[68] Not only does the friar's marriage plan set in motion a chain of events resulting in the deaths of Romeo and Juliet, the deaths of Mercutio and the County Paris also may be attributed in large part to his misguided belief that he can cure Verona's political problem.[69]

Not only does Friar Laurence lack the competence needed to successfully manage his political agenda, his treatment of the Christian doctrines of love and mercy are theoretically suspect as well. The Bible's teaching on mercy does not appear to support the friar's interpretation of its political utility.

---

[66] SHAKESPEARE, *supra* note 1, at Prologue, 10–11.
[67] SHAKESPEARE, *supra* note 1, at 3.5.140-197.
[68] SHAKESPEARE, *supra* note 1, at 1.1.1-37; 1.3.63-103.
[69] As noted earlier, had the Prince carried out the law and executed Romeo for killing Tybalt, the unnecessary death of Paris would never have occurred. But it is also the case that Paris would never have been at the Capulets' tomb, or fought with Romeo, had it not been for the friar's marriage plan and his subsequent plan to fake the death of Juliet.

The Bible's focus is upon mercy's healing effect on the individual souls of believers and how believers are to treat their fellow man in the daily workings of their lives. Both Old and New Testaments teach that the Lord is a merciful God.[70] The New Testament reveals how God's mercy will assume its ultimate form when Christ's teaching and, ultimately, his death bring salvation to mankind.[71] Believers are to show mercy to their fellow men in the course of their daily lives.[72]

Moreover, mercy is not said to supplant justice, but to accompany it: "And what does the Lord require of you? To act justly and to love mercy and to walk humbly with your God."[73] Or as the prophet Zechariah instructed: "And the word of the Lord came again to Zechariah: 'This is what the Lord Almighty says: "Administer true justice; show mercy and compassion to one another."'"[74] The New Testament, where the advent of Christ and his love is understood to complete the law of the Old Testament, does not abandon the concept of justice and mercy as complementary rather than at odds with one another: "Woe to you, teachers of the law and Pharisees, you hypocrites! You give a tenth of your spices—mint, dill and cumin. But you have neglected the more important matters of the law—justice, mercy and faithfulness."[75] One is hard-pressed to find Biblical passages instructing political authorities to forego justice or just laws in favor of mercy. Indeed, central to the teaching of the New Testament concerning Christ's purpose on earth involves his death as the necessary price or ransom for the forgiveness of the sins of mankind.[76] This, Paul says, was a matter of justice: "[God] did this to demonstrate his justice."[77] Mercy and justice appear to work together in God's plan as presented in scripture.[78] They are not separated. Christ received no pardon from God. Considering this scriptural background, and given his depiction of Friar Laurence's failed effort to utilize the doctrines of love and mercy as political tools rather than spiritual

[70] *See, e.g.*, Deuteronomy 4:31, 9:18; Nehemiah 9:31; Psalms 77:9; Jeremiah 3:12; Daniel 9:9; 2Samuel 24:14; 1Chronicles 21:13; Luke 1:50; Romans 9:18; 1Peter 1:3; Psalms 25:6, 28:6; Micah 7:18.

[71] *See, e.g.*, Jude 21; 1Peter 1:3.

[72] *See, e.g.*, Matthew 5:7, 9:13, 18:33; Luke 6:36; Jas 2:13; Jude 22-23; Hebrews 3:2.

[73] Micah 6:8.

[74] Zechariah 7:8-9.

[75] Matthew 23:23.

[76] *See, e.g.*, Romans 3:22-26.

[77] *See, e.g.*, Romans 3:25.

[78] *See, e.g.,* THOMAS AQUINAS, *The Summa Thelogica* , *in* THE BASIC WRITINGS OF ST. THOMAS AQUINAS 227 (Anton C. Pegis ed., 1945). In the words of Thomas Aquinas: "God acts mercifully, not indeed by going against His justice, but by doing something more than justice."

counsels, Shakespeare appears to be illustrating the corrosive effect of the Church's foray into ecclesiastical politics. But the friar's machinations are not yet complete.

Once Friar Laurence learns from Juliet of the plans to have her married to Paris, and that she intends to commit suicide rather than go through with the marriage, he is forced to devise a second plan—one far more "desperate" than the marriage plan.[79] For Christians the incarnation of love is Christ, and the friar takes his cue from this central tenet of his faith. Because of the friar's scheme, Juliet will imitate Christ by spending 42 hours in the tomb.[80] Thus, Friar Laurence devises his 'resurrection plan' once his marriage plan has gone awry. Critical to the success of this second plan is informing Romeo that Juliet is not really dead. The messenger, Friar John, does not deliver the letter to Romeo because a report of the plague delayed his "speed to Mantua." Had the messenger been Balthasar, as he promised Romeo it would be, there appears no reason why the letter would not have been successfully delivered.[81]

Moreover, we learn that Friar Laurence neglected to tell the busy Friar John how important the letter was, such that if delayed, he should make alternate arrangements to get word to Romeo (or Friar Laurence).[82] It is only now when it is too late, because Romeo was told that Juliet is dead, that Friar Laurence alerts Friar John to the importance of the message: "By my brotherhood / The letter was not nice, but full of charge / Of dear import; and the neglecting it / May do much danger."[83] Instead of recognizing his own negligence in failing to take the necessary precautions, Friar Laurence blames "[u]nhappy Fortune" and "these accidents."[84] He is equally willing to lay the blame at heaven's feet, rather than accept his own considerable part in the unhappy outcome of events, as he laments to Juliet in the scene in the Capulet tomb: "A greater power than we can contradict / Hath thwarted our intents."[85] His efforts to write Romeo a second time will be too late, and his plan's consequences now play out at the Capulets' tomb with the death of Paris at Romeo's hand, as well as the suicides of Romeo and Juliet.

---

[79] SHAKESPEARE, *supra* note 1, at 4.1.69-70.

[80] BLOOM, *supra* note 6, at 294.

[81] SHAKESPEARE, *supra* note 1, at 2.3.169–71.

[82] *See* Bert Cardullo, *The Friar's Flaw, the Play's Tragedy; The Experiment of Romeo and Juliet*, 28 CLA J. 408 (1984-1985). Cardullo notes the friar's lack of prudence as well in his essay: "Friars Laurence's rashness is responsible for Friar John's detention, not chance . . . It is the Friar's fault that Balthasar is unaware of her feigned death."

[83] SHAKESPEARE, *supra* note 1, at 5.2.17–19.

[84] SHAKESPEARE, *supra* note 1, at 5.2.17, 25.

[85] SHAKESPEARE, *supra* note 1, at 5.3.153 -154.

More shocking than his imprudence, however, is Friar Laurence's cowardice. He fears being discovered as the architect of the events leading to the scene in the tomb.[86] His cowardice leads him to flee the tomb—he "dare no longer stay"--even though he knows that Juliet will probably kill herself once he leaves.[87] He is later found trembling, sighing, and weeping.[88] The more one looks at the kindly and well-meaning friar, the more flawed he appears. These deaths are not the result of accidents. They are the product of Friar Laurence unwisely seeking to control Verona's political landscape.

The influence of the Church's teaching on mercy led the Prince to forgo the dictates of the law, thereby contributing to the deaths of those who might not otherwise have died. As the Church's representative, Friar Laurence fully endorses the Prince's preference for mercy over the strict form of justice mandated by Verona's laws. He upbraids Romeo for failing to appreciate the mercy of the Prince's exiling rather than executing him: "Thy fault our law calls death; but the kind Prince / Taking thy part, hath rushed aside the law / And turned that black word 'death' to banishment / This is dear mercy, and thou seest it not."[89] Whereas the Prince employs mercy as a political tool, the friar employs mercy's complement, which is love, as the instrument to perform his political craft.

The friar's resurrection plan also fits in with his understanding of the political utility of mercy. The new plan will utilize other central Christian doctrines to advance the friar's political agenda, specifically consciousness of sinfulness, atonement, and reconciliation. Once the marriage plan failed, the friar was forced to come up with this other, more radical plan to avoid the forced marriage to Paris that will likely result in Juliet's suicide. The friar may also continue to entertain hope that he can still salvage his plan to cure Verona's factionalism. Why did the friar choose this plan?

We recall that after Romeo had been banished, the friar instructed him to go to Mantua "where thou shalt live till we can find a time / To blaze your marriage, reconcile your friends / Beg pardon of the Prince, and call thee back / With twenty hundred thousand times more joy / Than thou went'st

---

[86] *See* GERRY BRENNER, *Shakespeare's Politically Ambitious Friar*, *in* SHAKESPEARE STUDIES 47-58, (vol. 13 1980) (including a helpful analysis of Friar Laurence's motives, "however, fails to appreciate the extent to which the friar represents the agenda of the Catholic Church, rather than his own interests more narrowly defined)

[87] SHAKESPEARE, *supra* note 1, at 5.3.159-60.

[88] SHAKESPEARE, *supra* note 1, at 5.3.184.

[89] SHAKESPEARE, *supra* note 1, at 3.3.24–27.

forth in lamentation."[90] Surely, it would be easier to secret Juliet away to Mantua to join Romeo immediately, rather than construct this elaborate resurrection ruse. The friar realizes that such a course not only would likely subject Romeo and Juliet to a life of poverty and exile, but it would also destroy his hope to save the city from itself. Friar Laurence would be exposed as a lawless meddler, disdainful of the families' concerns, rather than a "reverend holy friar" to whom "the whole city is much bound."[91] Instead, he must prepare the ground before revealing his role in the matter by manipulating the families' grief and guilt. By so doing, the friar hopes to diffuse the anger the families would turn toward him as well as retain the moral high ground he enjoys as a holy man. The friar believes only something evoking the meaning and effect of Christ's death on believers reenacted through Juliet may salvage his own reputation as well as his hope to reconcile the families.

What are the components of Friar Laurence's more radical resurrection plan? First, Christ died to atone for the sins of mankind. Accordingly, this second plan has the advantage of reminding the Capulets of their own sinfulness, for which the vicarious death of the Juliet-Christ is required to atone.[92] Consciousness of sin and guilt, the friar knows from his faith, undermines pride and hatred. Romeo's banishment has already chastened the Montagues, with Lady Montague having died because of her grief over her son's exile.[93] The friar must now work on the Capulets, and he does not hesitate to remind them of their sinful behavior. As they grieve Juliet's apparent death, Friar Laurence chastises the Capulets for the selfish, political motivation that caused them to seek their daughter's marriage with Paris: "The most you sought was her promotion / For 'twas your heaven she should be advanced."[94] The friar then suggests to the Capulets that they are responsible in some manner for Juliet's death: "The heavens do low'r upon you for some ill / Move them no more by crossing their high will."[95] Of course, since Juliet remains alive, this is a blatant lie, but one that is useful in sowing the seeds of guilt in the souls of the Capulets. The friar is a

[90] SHAKESPEARE, *supra* note 1, at 3.3.150–54.

[91] SHAKESPEARE, *supra* note 1, at 4.2.31–32.

[92] WEINBERGER, *supra* note 6, at 368. Weinberger argues, somewhat differently, that Friar Laurence's goal in staging the fake resurrection is to "punish" the Capulets through Juliet's death, in order to "prepare them for a gratitude that could overwhelm their sense of political loss and reconcile them to the connection with the Montagues. . . ." A continuing sense of sinfulness, I would contend, is both more central to Christian teaching than punishment, as well as the more effective antidote to pride.

[93] SHAKESPEARE, *supra* note 1, at 5.3.210–11.

[94] SHAKESPEARE, *supra* note 1, at 4.5.71–72.

[95] SHAKESPEARE, *supra* note 1, at 4.5.94–95.

liar, but he defended himself on the grounds that the good that his latest plan will accomplish justifies his actions. In his own words: "vice [is] sometime's by action dignified."[96]

Second, Christian doctrine holds that Christ's resurrection defeated hatred and death, bringing peace and joy to those who believe in him. Similarly, the joy the Capulets will experience once they realize she is not dead—her "resurrection"—combined with the consciousness of their own sinfulness, would undermine the pride and hatred that forms the basis for the factional discord. Of course, the fact that Juliet is alive must be revealed. Empty tombs are not easily explained. Moreover, we know that Lady Capulet had a spy in Mantua.[97] The friar is gambling that the Capulets will be reminded of the mystery of the resurrection and atonement once Juliet is revived, and that this will evoke humble gratitude on their part. He is gambling that this gratitude will mingle with their guilt, of which he has reminded them, and lead them not only to excuse the friar's interference but also embrace reconciliation with the Montagues. Such is Friar Laurence's "desperate" "hope."[98]

As Shakespeare referenced in the Prologue, and the friar fails to grasp, the successful reconciliation (even if only temporary) of the families requires Juliet's actual, not feigned, death. In fact, it requires the actual death of both children. Indeed, it is likely that had the Capulets discovered that Juliet was never really dead, their happiness would have been tempered, and their consciousness of guilt removed, such that reconciliation with the Montagues would not have transpired. With the lovers' deaths dies the friar's scheme, but only in part. The necessary consciousness of sin and accompanying guilt brought on by the friar's machinations remain. Indeed, the guilt is increased as the parents recognize the lovers' (and Juliet's in particular) dedication to love and come to see the sinfulness of their own petty hatreds in that light. The pious Prince drives this point home, extolling the children's "course of love" and condemning the families' unchristian hatred: "See what a scourge is laid upon your hate / That heaven finds means to kill your joys with love."[99] As Shakespeare told us at the beginning of the play, the sanction, the reality of death, is necessary to control and subdue the most destructive political passions. Religious sanction may increase guilt and undermine pride, but in the end, death is required to subdue this kind of factional discord. Only now are Montague and Capulet ready to reconcile.

---

[96] SHAKESPEARE, *supra* note 1, at 2.3.22.
[97] SHAKESPEARE, *supra* note 1, at 3.5.88–93.
[98] SHAKESPEARE, *supra* note 1, at 4.1.68–70.
[99] SHAKESPEARE, *supra* note 1, at 5.3.287, 282–93.

While Shakespeare presents Friar Laurence as meddlesome, imprudent, and cowardly, he does not present him as a vicious man in any way. Gerry Brenner's depiction of the friar as "prompted by self-aggrandizing ambitions that are equal to, if not stronger than, those in Capulet and Prince Escalus" is misplaced to the extent that it understands the friar as acting out of a desire for self-promotion.[100] Rather, Friar Laurence truly believes that he is advancing the good of Verona. In this way he serves the Church and its effort to control the political landscape, but he does so with "good intentions."

Justice is lacking in Verona as familial tribalism dominates. The weak Prince is certainly not the answer, but neither is Friar Laurence in his effort to provide a political cure, first in the form of Christian love, and then in the form of consciousness of sin. He politicizes what should remain non-political and neglects his proper office of tending to his flock's spiritual needs. The friar might have exerted his influence on the individual citizens' attitudes toward one another by counseling them against misguided ambition, pride, and anger, and encouraging them in the name of love and forgiveness. In fact, he seems more interested in politics and philosophy. While he does suggest Romeo consult the consolations of philosophy, Friar Laurence never recommends prayer or attention to matters of faith to Romeo when the young lover is bemoaning his banishment from Verona.

Romeo, Juliet, Mercutio, Paris, Lady Montague, and perhaps even Tybalt, are all dead in large part due to Friar Laurence's effort to resolve Verona's factionalism. His effort has been to control, even transform, vicious political passions by means of his Christian doctrines of mercy, love, and consciousness of sin. His efforts have only led to more death. Friar Laurence conflates the city of God and the city of man. In so doing, he neglects the teaching on eternity that properly attends the former, while undermining the proper attention to the temporal realities that rightly attend the latter. Friar Laurence "should be devout," but Dante and Shakespeare agree he is not.[101] Shakespeare would also appear to agree, at least in part, with Machiavelli's stinging rebuke that "[t]he first debt which we, Italians, owe to the Church and to priests, therefore, is that we have become irreligious and perverse."[102] The solution must be a political one, whereby the law and justice are respected and enforced in cities where public honor and a sense of national pride prevail in due course. The friar's misuse of

---

[100] BRENNER, *supra* note 86, at 48.
[101] DANTE, *supra* note 53, at 6.85.
[102] MACHIAVELLI, *supra* note 41, at 1:12.

Christian love, however, is not the whole of the story Shakespeare is telling us on the subject.

Romeo and the Law of Love

In her musings on her balcony, Juliet asks: "Wherefore art thou Romeo?"[103] Who is Romeo? The easy answer is that supplied by Mercutio: "[y]ou are a lover."[104] Indeed, Romeo is a deeply erotic soul, consumed with the idea of love. Romeo's fixation with love supplies cynical Mercutio with opportunities to ridicule his friend: "Romeo! humors! madman! passion! lover! / Appear thou in the likeness of a sigh; / Speak but one rhyme, and I am satisfied!"[105] Romeo is also a Christian, or at least shaped by the Christianity of his day as it has come down from Saint Peter's Church and his teacher, Friar Laurence. As such, Romeo accepts Christianity's teaching concerning the absolute superiority of love, but he fails to keep divine and human love within their proper spheres, creating in Juliet the object of his religion of love. Romeo's confusion concerning divine and human love is reflected in his initial discourse with Benvolio when he expresses his belief in the contradictory character of reality, and, in particular, of love. He does so in a way that includes theological themes such as chaos, creation, and human vanity: "Why then, O brawling love, O loving hate / O anything, of nothing first create! / O heavy lightness, serious vanity / Misshapen chaos of well-seeming forms."[106] These remarks follow Romeo's observation of the results of the initial fight between the families, when he cryptically remarks: "Here's much to do with hate, but more with love."[107] Romeo may simply be saying that the families' hatred flows from the excesses of their own self-love. Shakespeare may, however, be indicating through Romeo's comment the deeper issue of the problematic manner in which love is understood in an Italy dominated politically and theologically by the Catholic Church.

In any discussion of love it is helpful to consider its close kinship to Eros, or erotic longing. As the son of Aphrodite in Greek mythology, Eros was

---

103 SHAKESPEARE, *supra* note 1, at 2.2.48.
104 SHAKESPEARE, *supra* note 1, at 1.4.17.
105 SHAKESPEARE, *supra* note 1, at 2.1.7 – 9.
106 SHAKESPEARE, *supra* note 1, at 1.1.174–77.
107 SHAKESPEARE, *supra* note 1, at 1.1.173.

the god of love. On one level, Eros represented sexual love or desire.[108] One can desire many other things, obviously, not all of them praiseworthy. In classical thought, however, Eros transcends unworthy desires, and even sexual desire, because of Eros' preoccupation with the beautiful. In Plato's Symposium, it is Diotima who gives us this classical account of Eros, as she tells Socrates:

> Such is the right approach or induction to love-matters. Beginning
>
> from obvious beauties he must for the sake of that highest beauty
>
> be ever climbing aloft, as on the rungs of a ladder, from one to two, and from two to all beautiful bodies; from personal beauty he proceeds to beautiful observances, from observance to beautiful learning, and from learning at last to that particular study which is concerned with the beautiful itself and that alone; so that in the end he comes to know the very essence of beauty. In that state of life above all others, my dear Socrates, said the Mantinean woman, a man finds it truly worthwhile to live, as he contemplates essential beauty.[109]

On a deeper level, erotic longing, particularly for the beautiful, is said to represent the desire to achieve completeness or wholeness. As Allan Bloom has put it in his analysis of the Symposium: "Eros is desire and . . . one desires only what one lacks."[110] In other words, Eros is that desire which is born by the recognition of incompleteness, and the corresponding desire to be complete. In this highest sense of the term, Eros represents the desire for the beautiful which ultimately seeks the perfection that humans lack in this imperfect world. This teaching is not inconsistent with our common sense awareness of the effect of beauty. Only those determined to follow the analysis of modern scientific reductionism would deny the intimations of completeness, even eternity, brought on by the experience of the beautiful. Certainly pre-moderns such as Wordsworth, to cite but one example, were fully attuned to beauty's power:

---

[108] THE NEW OXFORD AMERICAN DICTIONARY 573 (2d ed. 2005).

[109] Plato's Symposium, Loeb Classical Library, Harvard University Press, 1967 edition. W.R.M. Lamb trans. 211c 1-211d4.

[110] BLOOM, *supra* note 6, at 498.

And I have felt
A presence that disturbs me with the joy
Of elevated thoughts; a sense sublime
Of something far more deeply interfused,
Whose dwelling is the light of setting suns,
And the round ocean and the living air,
And the blue sky, and in the mind of man:
A motion and a spirit, that impels
All thinking things, all objects of all thought,
And rolls through all things. Therefore am I still
A lover of the meadows and the woods,
And mountains; and of all that we behold
From this green earth . . .[111]

Is the erotic Romeo also a lover of the beautiful in the sense just described?

It is clear Romeo has many excellent qualities that compare as favorably, if not more favorably, to any other major figure in the play. Even his enemy, Capulet, acknowledges his reputation throughout Verona as a gentlemanly young man: "And, to say truth, Verona brags of him / To be a virtuous and well-governed youth."[112] The friendships of men like Benvolio and Mercutio also speak well of Romeo. Mercutio clearly intends, in his confrontation with Tybalt, to save his friend even if it costs Mercutio his own life.[113] As to intellectual ability, Romeo is the superior even of clever Mercutio. In their battle of wits, Mercutio acknowledges defeat: "Come between us, good Benvolio! / My wits faint."[114] Thus, while Romeo may justly earn Mercutio's mockery because he is a "madman" in his all-consuming preoccupation with love, he is not to be simply dismissed as a man without superior qualities.

Romeo recognizes that participation in Verona's public life offers little more than attachment to the petty quarrels of noble families nursing "ancient grudge[s]," the causes of which are no longer even remembered.[115] He has

---

[111] WILLIAM WORDSWORTH, Lines Composed a Few Miles Above Tintern Abbey On Revisiting the Banks of the Wye During a Tour. July 13, 1798, *in* THE NORTON ANTHOLOGY OF ENGLISH LITERATURE 157 (W.W. Norton & Co., Inc. 1970).
[112] SHAKESPEARE, *supra* note 1, at 1.1.67-68.
[113] Mercutio knows that Tybalt intends to kill Romeo and will likely succeed. In order to save his friend, Mercutio attempts to divert Tybalt's anger toward himself and away from Romeo, only to have Romeo's intervention in his efforts lead to his own death.
[114] SHAKESPEARE, *supra* note 1, at 2.4.66–67.
[115] SHAKESPEARE, *supra* note 1, at Prologue, 3.

"heard it all."[116] Neither is he interested in the life of detached cynicism represented by Mercutio. Friar Laurence encourages him to embrace another kind of life available to those who inhabit his Christian state: the life of philosophic contemplation.[117] None of these alternatives appeal to Romeo's youthful and erotic soul.

Romeo is certainly an erotic soul by nature. But if his extreme love of love were solely, or decidedly the product of his unique nature, then Romeo would truly be Mercutio's "madman." And there would be nothing to learn about the nature of love from madmen. Accordingly, and as has been suggested earlier, his eroticism is influenced by the state of civic life in Verona as well. This essay has argued that Verona's civic life, in turn, results from the Catholic Church's intrusion into the political realm and corresponding abdication of its proper role in the tending of the spiritual needs of its flock, as well as the Church's refusal to grant to the political virtues their proper dignity. Romeo rejects the shallow, unsatisfying life offered by Veronese politics in favor of the life of erotic love. And Romeo's contempt for the world as he sees it only makes his turn to erotic love all the more extreme.

Ultimately, Romeo's eroticism leads him to love what he believes love promises more than he loves Juliet as an actual person. Moments before seeing Juliet at the Capulet party and falling hopelessly in "love" with her, he was just as hopelessly in "love" with Rosaline.[118] But it is the ladies' beauty that truly moves Romeo's heart. While he knows absolutely nothing of Juliet's character, her beauty moves him to "love" her: "[d]id my heart love till now? Forswear it, sight / For I ne'er saw true beauty till this night."[119] In Romeo's eyes, Juliet represents a "Beauty too rich for use, for earth too dear."[120] It is a form of beauty that for Romeo far transcends the lowly things of this world. As with his "love" of Rosaline, just prior to his being captured by Juliet's beauty, Romeo was hopelessly under the spell of Rosaline's beauty: "O, she is rich in beauty; only poor / That, when she dies, with beauty dies her store."[121]

Romeo's friend, Benvolio, knows physical beauty by itself cannot sustain any serious form of love and so correctly predicts that the object of

[116] SHAKESPEARE, *supra* note 1, at 1.1.172.
[117] SHAKESPEARE, *supra* note 1, at 3.3.54–56.
[118] SHAKESPEARE, *supra* note 1, at 1.5.52.
[119] SHAKESPEARE, *supra* note 1, at 1.5.52–53.
[120] SHAKESPEARE, *supra* note 1, at 1.5.46.
[121] SHAKESPEARE, *supra* note 1, at 1.1.213 – 214.

Romeo's erotic desire will prove quite changeable: "Tut! You saw her fair, none else being by, / Herself poised with herself in either eye; / But in that crystal scales let there be weighed / Your lady's love against some other maid / That I will show you shining at this feast, / And she shall scant show well that now seems best."[122] While doing exactly as Benvolio forecasts by easily replacing his obsession with Rosaline's beauty with that of Juliet, Romeo never comes to understand his own fickleness. Even upon his (mistaken) discovery of Juliet's death at play's end, much of Romeo's heartbreak is expressed in the form of a poetic figuration of a battle between Juliet's beauty and death itself: "Death, that hath sucked the honey of thy breath, / Hath no power yet upon thy beauty. / Thou are not conquered. Beauty's ensign yet / Is crimson in thy lips and in thy cheeks, / And death's pale flag is not advanced there."[123] The Chorus' sarcastic appraisal of the fickle quality of Romeo's love provides a stark contrast to his beautiful speeches at the Capulet party that immediately precede the appraisal:

> Now old desire doth in his deathbed lie,
> And young affection gapes to be his heir;
> That fair for which love groaned for and would die,
> With tender Juliet matched, is now not fair.
> Now Romeo is beloved and loves again,
> Alike bewitched by the charm of looks . . . .[124]

Romeo's erotic love is engaged above all by the physical beauty he sees first in Rosaline, and later in Juliet. To a certain extent, then, Romeo remains on the lower rung of Diotima's ladder of love. But Juliet's perfect beauty—a beauty which is "for earth too dear"—also represents for Romeo the desire for completeness or perfection that he finds so lacking in Verona.

Romeo's conception of love and beauty, however, is also influenced by his Christian religion. Christianity teaches the superiority of love to all other things.[125] Love is the fundamental stuff of existence, the sum and substance of all that is highest, best, and most beautiful in heaven and on earth; it is

[122] SHAKESPEARE, *supra* note 1, at 1.2.96 -101.
[123] SHAKESPEARE, *supra* note 1, at 5.3.92 – 96.
[124] SHAKESPEARE, *supra* note 1, at 2.1–6.
[125] 1 Cor. 13:13.

God Himself.[126] The merely human pales by comparison, as the world is full of sin and perishable:

> Do not love the world or anything in the world. If anyone loves the world, the love of the Father is not in him. For everything in the world—the cravings of sinful man, the lust in his eyes and the boasting of what he has and does—comes not from the Father but from the world. The world and its desires pass away, but the man who does the will of God lives forever.[127]

The centrality accorded love in the teaching of Romeo's Christian faith is consistent with the importance of love to a naturally erotic soul such as Romeo. But Juliet too is a Christian, and her understanding of love assumes a firmer, more grounded form than Romeo's. Is it the case that Romeo interprets his faith's teaching in a manner different from Juliet's understanding? What in the Christian teaching about love may lend itself to the excesses we find in the kind of love Romeo comes to embrace?

In addition to the verses just cited from 1 John—which appear to demean worldly things when compared with God's glory—there is an antinomian strain in Scripture that suggests the law is unneeded or superfluous for the believer. This strain is particularly evident in St. Paul's teaching in Romans.[128] The law is superfluous for believers because God's Grace has conquered sin in their hearts—those who do not sin do not need the law: "For sin shall not be your master, because you are not under law, but under grace."[129] As will be argued, Romeo's conception of love is similarly lawless in that it transcends the things of this world. Juliet's beauty represents the saving grace that will deliver Romeo from his despair. Romeo's love reflects that train in Christianity that offers the fulfillment of an antinomian erotic longing.

As discussed earlier, there is also a significant aspect of Christian doctrine that counsels respect for the things properly belonging to Caesar. This interpretation of Scripture's teaching on Mercy does not appear consistent with that of Friar Laurence or the Prince, but it is arguably more in line with

---

126 2 Cor. 13:11, 1 John 4: 16.
127 1 John 2:15 - 17.
128 Romans 3:19 – 23, 4:13 – 15, 6:14, 10:4.
129 Romans 6:14.

traditional notions of justice. Friar Laurence, Romeo's spiritual advisor and the Catholic Church's agent, however, would rather control what belongs to Caesar than render unto Caesar what is Caesar's. Justice is Caesar's, but the friar will seek to supplant traditional notions of justice with his own understanding, based on love and mercy. Once the influence of Friar Laurence comes to dominate the spiritual landscape, Eros is left without an alternative to otherworldly attachments. The comings and goings of this world have largely lost their charm. Accordingly, the particular form of love Romeo comprehends reflects contempt for the things of this world—Juliet's "[b]eauty" is "too rich for use, for earth too dear."[130]

Romeo's erotic imagination is thoroughly shaped by Christian images. His first expressions about and to Juliet at the Capulet party include more than occasional references to heavenly things: they are a veritable love prayer containing repeated references to holy Christian themes and symbols. Juliet is a "dear saint," and her hand is a "holy shrine."[131] The touch of her hand will "make blessed my rude hand."[132] His own lips are "two blushing pilgrims," which stand ready to "pray" by kissing Juliet, "lest faith turn to despair."[133] When Romeo does kiss her, he pronounces that it is his "prayer's effect I take."[134] The kiss, rather than true prayer, removes sin: "Thus from my lips, by thine my sin is purged."[135] In the transport of Romeo's erotic imaginings, Juliet figuratively assumes the role Christianity reserves for Christ. In the famous balcony scene, Romeo continues his worship of Juliet. She is a "dear saint" a "bright angel" a "winged messenger of heaven" whose eyes are two "of the fairest stars in all the heaven."[136] Again, Romeo alludes to Juliet's capacity to absolve him of sin through her love: "[c]all me but love, and I'll be new baptized / Henceforth I never will be Romeo."[137] These religiously laden love speeches are more than poetic excess or hyperbole. For Romeo, love becomes a religious transport by which he may escape the limitations of this poor world and is divorced from any form of earthly wisdom: "[l]ove goes toward love as schoolboys from

---

[130] SHAKESPEARE, *supra* note 1, at 1.5.47. Romeo displays his contempt for earthly life throughout the play. See, e.g., SHAKESPEARE, *supra* note 1, at 1.4.110; 5.1.62; 5.1.81; 5.3.112.

[131] SHAKESPEARE, *supra* note 1, at 1.5.103, 94.

[132] SHAKESPEARE, *supra* note 1, at 1.5.51.

[133] SHAKESPEARE, *supra* note 1, at 1.5.95, 104.

[134] SHAKESPEARE, *supra* note 1, at 1.5.105.

[135] SHAKESPEARE, *supra* note 1, at 1.5.107.

[136] SHAKESPEARE, *supra* note 1, at 1.5.107, at 2.2.57, 26, 28, 15.

[137] SHAKESPEARE, *supra* note 1, at 2.2.51–52.

their books / But love from love, toward school with heavy looks."[138] As noted earlier, Romeo rejects the consolation of philosophy and its insights.

When confronted with the Prince's banishment decree, Romeo violently rejects the sentence because it separates him from Juliet. Juliet's presence constitutes heaven itself: "[h]eaven is here / Where Juliet lives."[139] Even carrion flies "steal immortal blessings from her lips."[140] Juliet represents immortality in Romeo's eyes. As for the word "banishment," the "damned use that word in hell / Howling attends it."[141] Of course, for Christians the damned use the word "banishment" because they are forever separated from God's presence. Later Romeo muses on a dream in which "I dreamt my lady came and found me dead / … and breathed such life with kisses in my lips / That I revived and was an emperor."[142] Once again, Romeo substitutes Juliet for divine love, for Christ.

Romeo's contempt for the world and worldly wisdom that shapes his longing for a trans-political life of idealized love brings him perilously close to nihilism.[143] When he learns of his love's apparent death he has no recourse to any form of reasoned understanding, and he declares, "I defy you stars!"[144] The radical disjunction, in Romeo's mind, between earthly life and heavenly love necessarily rejects any intelligible compatibility between the two, pushing him toward nihilistic despair. In his own words, Romeo is "life-weary"[145] and ready to escape "[f]rom this world-wearied flesh"[146] which bears the burden of a fate that is at best indifferent to his sufferings ("the yoke of inauspicious stars."[147]) Romeo abandons consideration of eternal life, choosing instead to make the tomb he shares with Juliet his place of "everlasting rest."[148]

Moreover, by choosing the trans-political life of love, Romeo partially emulates Friar Laurence when the Franciscan seeks to resolve Verona's factionalism through a resort to love. Tybalt represents the continuation of

---

[138] SHAKESPEARE, *supra* note 1, at 2.2.157–158.
[139] SHAKESPEARE, *supra* note 1, at 3.3.29–30.
[140] SHAKESPEARE, *supra* note 1, at 3.3.37.
[141] SHAKESPEARE, *supra* note 1, at 3.3.47–48.
[142] SHAKESPEARE, *supra* note 1, at 5.1.6–9.
[143] The rejection of all religious and moral principles, often in the belieft that life is meaningless. THE NEW OXFORD AMERICAN DICTIONARY 1151 (2d ed. 2005).
[144] SHAKESPEARE, *supra* note 1, at 5.1.24.
[145] SHAKESPEARE, *supra* note 1, at 5.1.62.
[146] SHAKESPEARE, *supra* note 1, at 5.3.112.
[147] SHAKESPEARE, *supra* note 1, at 5.3.111.
[148] SHAKESPEARE, *supra* note 1, at 5.3.110.

this factionalism more acutely than any character in the play. While Mercutio understands that the only effective way to deal with Tybalt is to defeat him by means of force, Romeo seeks to overcome Tybalt's hatred through love. Romeo interferes in the fight between Mercutio and Tybalt, leading to Tybalt's stabbing Mercutio under Romeo's arm. This is well-meaning foolishness on Romeo's part, brought on by the secret marriage which causes Romeo to try to placate his implacable new kinsman. In so doing, Romeo has (momentarily) become servant to the friar's plan, seeking to quench political discord by appeals to love: "I do protest I never injured thee / But love thee better than thou canst devise / Till thou shalt know the reason of my love / And so, good Capulet, which name I tender / As dearly as my own, be satisfied."[149] Mercutio blames his friend for his death: "[w]hy the devil came you between us? / I was hurt under your arm."[150] Foreshadowing the friar's explanation to the Prince concerning his role in the events that led to the deaths at the tomb, Romeo can only reply: "I thought all for the best." [151] Both intended that love rule over discord, and both brought more death because of their good intentions. The similarity between Romeo and the friar ends there, for apart from the fight with Tybalt, Romeo is not interested in resolving political problems. Rather, he is interested in transcending them altogether.

This essay argues that Prince Escalus, Friar Laurence, and Romeo suffer from the Church's misguided teaching on love. But it is one thing for Shakespeare to draw our attention to the pre-reformation Church's distortion of the proper relationship between human and divine love. It is quite another to discern in Romeo & Juliet a blueprint for a healthy model of that relationship. In the character of Juliet, however, the outlines of such a model may be found.

Juliet: Christian Love Reconsidered

In The Four Loves, C.S. Lewis considered and contrasted Eros and Christian Love.[152] According to Lewis, the highest form of love is Christian Charity, followed in descending order by Eros, Friendship and, finally,

---

149 SHAKESPEARE, *supra* note 1, at 3.1.67–71.
150 SHAKESPEARE, *supra* note 1, at 3.1.100–01.
151 SHAKESPEARE, *supra* note 1, at 3.1.102.
152 C.S. LEWIS, THE FOUR LOVES (Harcourt Brace & Co. 1988).

Affection. Eros, of course, includes sexual attraction and activity.[153] In fact, according to Lewis, sexual union often is a frustrated attempt to realize a more complete union urged upon us by Eros.[154] This frustrating quality of seeking to employ the vehicle of the body to realize something beyond what the body can deliver, however, can assume the form of a transcendent endeavor: "The longing for a union which only the flesh can mediate while the flesh, our mutually excluding bodies, renders it forever unattainable can have the grandeur of a metaphysical pursuit."[155] To fall prey to this divinization of sexual Eros is to court false gods, Lewis warns, identifying past examples such as "'the Pagan sacrament' in sex."[156] Lewis follows Plato's classical interpretation of Eros set forth in The Symposium insofar as Eros encompasses, but ultimately surpasses mere sexual desire alone: "Sexual desire, without Eros, wants it, the thing in itself; Eros wants the Beloved."[157] But even though Eros is not irretrievably linked to sex, Lewis maintains, it nevertheless can become a religion of love on its own; and this constitutes yet another form of false religion: "And yet it cannot, just as it stands, be the voice of God Himself. For Eros, speaking with that very grandeur and displaying that very transcendence of self, may urge to evil as well as to good."[158] Lewis offers the following description of someone who submits to this false religion:

> But Eros, honoured without reservation and obeyed unconditionally, becomes a demon. And this is just how he claims to be honoured and obeyed. Divinely indifferent to our selfishness, he is demonically rebellious to every claim of God or man that would oppose him.[159]

Lewis' description comports well with Shakespeare's depiction of Romeo, and we recognize such rebelliousness when, upon learning of his beautiful Juliet's (apparent) death, he exclaims: "Then I defy you stars!"[160] As discussed earlier, Romeo's nihilistic rejection of the laws of God or man are the product of his misguided love honoring and obeying Eros unconditionally. Romeo's unconditional love of the beauty he sees in Juliet, a love that cannot be sustained because it is attached to something (or someone) perishable, leads to his near demonic rejection of all authority. In

---

153 *Id.* at 91 – 107.
154 *Id.* at 102.
155 *Id.* at 102.
156 *Id.* at 103
157 *Id.* at 94.
158 LEWIS, *supra* note 152, at 108.
159 LEWIS, *supra* note 152, at 110.
160 SHAKESPEARE, *supra* note 1, at 5.1.24.

the classical understanding of Eros, Romeo fails to reach beyond personal beauty to that "study which is concerned with the beautiful itself and that alone."[161] In the understanding of Christian love presented by C.S. Lewis, Romeo has settled on worshipping a false god, and so cannot arrive at the highest of loves, Charity, or the love of God himself.[162]

In Juliet, unlike in Friar Laurence or in Romeo, Shakespeare presents us with a far fairer picture of a love, and in particular, Christian love.[163] Despite her youth, Juliet's understanding of love is far deeper and certainly more realistic than Romeo's. As will be argued, it also conforms more closely to traditional Christian doctrine. Juliet is passionate in her love, but her nature seems more grounded and less given to the erotic excesses that preoccupy the soul of Romeo. Moreover, as a woman of her time, the expectations she entertains of a full and happy life do not include the possibility of honorific political pursuits. Thus she is less likely than Romeo to feel the effects of an emasculated civic life.

Troubled by the difficulties presented by her love for the son of the rival family, Juliet reflects on Romeo's true nature as opposed to his family identity and expresses her willingness to reject her family for him: "O Romeo, Romeo! Wherefore art thou Romeo? / Deny thy father and refuse thy name / Or, if thou wilt not, be but sworn my love / And I'll no longer be a Capulet."[164] She concludes her famous "[w]hat's in a name" reverie, however, somewhat unrealistically by refusing to acknowledge the fact of one's association with a particular family (like one's association with a particular political order) is an integral part of who one is: "And for thy name, which is no part of thee / Take all myself."[165] Nevertheless, Juliet, far more than Romeo, is keenly attentive to the true conditions surrounding the course of their future love.

Upon first encountering Romeo at the feast prepared by her father, Juliet gently rebukes Romeo's passionate overtures by reference to Christian doctrine: "Good pilgrim, you do wrong your hand too much, / Which mannerly devotion shows in this; / For saints have hands that pilgrims'

---

161 Plato, Symposium 211c.
162 LEWIS, *supra* note 152, at 116.
163 Critics have noted the quality of Juliet's love generally speaking, without, however, identifying its Christian character. See, e.g., DAVID SCOTT KASTAN, *Introduction* to WILLIAM SHAKESPEARE, ROMEO AND JULIET 1, 9 (Mario DiGangi ed., Barnes & Noble, Inc. 2007). "In this [Juliet's] formulation, love no longer involves giving and taking, gaining and losing; instead, it has the miraculous power to produce infinite gain from infinite giving."
164 SHAKESPEARE, *supra* note 1, at 2.2.33–36.
165 SHAKESPEARE, *supra* note 1, at 2.2.48-49.

hands do touch, / And palm to palm is holy palmers' kiss."[166] Later, she repeatedly draws his attention to the dangers the families' hatred poses to their union.[167] She counters his flowery love speeches with cautions about the difference between true love and "light love," and rejects Romeo's vows of love altogether as insubstantial.[168] Just prior to their actual marriage, Juliet continues to upbraid Romeo gently and rejects his request that they take time to speak lovely words about their "imagined happiness."[169] Reality, not unchecked imagination, forms the foundation for real love: "Conceit, more rich in matter than in words / Brags of his substance, not of ornament."[170] Unlike Romeo, she recognizes that their mutual attraction is "too rash, too unadvised, too sudden / Too like the lightening, which doth cease to be / Ere one can say 'It lightens'."[171] Juliet realizes the passionate feelings she and Romeo share do not constitute a mature form of love, but are only a "bud of love" waiting to flower.[172]

In his interpretation of Measure for Measure, Harry Jaffa argues that Shakespeare is elucidating the importance of chastity (marital fidelity) as a salutary political principle because it supports strong families. Strong families, in turn, are essential for healthy political communities. The Vienna of Measure for Measure is dissolute in large part because it lacks such a political principle:

> [In Vienna] we do not see any families. Sexual desire may be sublimated or indulged. But we do not see sexual desire as an extension of self-preservation, and self-preservation extended to include the family, whence it is transformed into patriotism.[173]

In Verona, we do see families, but they do not appear healthy. Instead, they are factional—more concerned with advancing their own interests than those of their children or their country. As noted earlier, David Wagner argues that Romeo and Juliet undertake (without being aware of their

166 SHAKESPEARE, *supra* note 1, at 1.5.97 – 100.
167 SHAKESPEARE, *supra* note 1, at 2.2.64–65, 70, 74.
168 SHAKESPEARE, *supra* note 1, at 2.2.105, 113, 118.
169 SHAKESPEARE, *supra* note 1, at 2.6.28.
170 SHAKESPEARE, *supra* note 1, at 2.6.31–32.
171 SHAKESPEARE, *supra* note 1, at 2.2.118–120.
172 SHAKESPEARE, *supra* note 1, at 2.2.121.
173 HARRY V. JAFFA, Chastity as a Political Principle: An Interpretation of Shakespeare's *Measure for Measure*, *in* SHAKESPEARE AS A POLITICAL THINKER 182 (John Alvis & Thomas G. West eds., Carolina Academic Press 1981).

undertaking) the restoration of the civic order through their marriage based on spousal Eros, rather than the self-interested, patriarchal family ordering. While this is true in part, the erotic foundation of their attachment is only a piece of the puzzle. Juliet is a better Christian than the parents. Immediately after first meeting Romeo, Juliet's thoughts turn to marriage: "If he be married, / My grave is like to be my wedding bed."[174] In the orchard scene with Romeo, she is first to raise the subject of marriage as the proper culmination of their love, and is already planning the particular details of that marriage: "If that thy bent of love be honorable, / Thy purpose marriage, send me word tomorrow, / By one that I'll procure to come to thee, / Where and what time thou wilt perform the rite."[175] She later ties her marriage vows to her faith: "God joined my heart and Romeo's, thou our hands."[176] God's sanction of her marriage vow means everything to Juliet, and only Romeo's death can undo that sanction: "my husband is on earth, my faith in heaven / How shall that faith return again to earth / Unless that husband send it me from heaven / By leaving earth?"[177]

When her mother first raises the subject of marriage—even before she meets Romeo—Juliet associates the institution with honor: "It is an honor that I dream not of."[178] After learning she is to marry Paris, Juliet tells Friar Laurence she is willing to kill herself to "live an unstained wife to my sweet husband."[179] Juliet's suicide, otherwise considered a sin, must be understood in the context of her faithful commitment to remain "unstained." Actually, Juliet chooses to become a martyr to her holy vow. For Juliet, "true honor" and honorable action are associated with fidelity to holy marriage.[180] Were the cities of Italy populated by marriages made strong and secure by such Juliets, they would contribute toward the formation of healthy, patriotic political communities. The weak and divided Italy of Romeo and Juliet cannot sustain such marriages. They must await a different arrangement between church and state.

While aware of the difficulties and shortcomings of their mutual infatuation, Juliet also reveals the depths of her commitment to a love that fulfills her faith's tenets. After meeting Romeo, Juliet recognizes a potential conflict between her infatuation with him and her faith by acknowledging that

---

174 SHAKESPEARE, *supra* note 1, at 1.5.134 - 35.
175 SHAKESPEARE, *supra* note 1, at 2.2.143 - 146.
176 SHAKESPEARE, *supra* note 1, at 4.1.55.
177 SHAKESPEARE, *supra* note 1, at 3.5.207–210.
178 SHAKESPEARE, *supra* note 1, at 1.3.66.
179 SHAKESPEARE, *supra* note 1, at 4.1.88.
180 SHAKESPEARE, *supra* note 1, at 4.1.65.

Romeo has become "the god of my idolatry."[181] Juliet's reference to "idolatry" precedes her moving testimony of the nature of her love for Romeo. Her testimonial reflects an understanding of love that is far more in keeping with Christian teaching than is Romeo's erotic preoccupation: "And yet I wish but for the thing I have / My bounty is as boundless as the sea / My love as deep; the more I give to thee / The more I have, for both are infinite."[182] While tempering her love for Romeo with an awareness of it possibly becoming idolatrous, Juliet's heart bears a Christian stamp whereby she receives more by giving more. The universalism of her Christian love is reflected in Juliet's willingness to leave Italy and follow Romeo "throughout the world."[183] Notably, the Chorus does not subject Juliet's love to the degree of sarcasm it had leveled at Romeo's "young affection."[184]

In Juliet's attitude toward love, then, we find something approaching Lewis' depiction of the highest form of Christian love—Charity. Specifically, Juliet's claim that her love is defined by its character as a gift knowing neither limit nor bound resembles Lewis' description of Charity as "Gift-love."[185] Lewis identifies this "Gift-love" with the very essence of God's being: "God is love. Again, 'Herein is love, not that we loved God but that he loved us' (1 John IV, 10) . . . We begin at the real beginning, with love as the Divine energy. This primal love is Gift-love. In God there is no hunger that needs to be filled, only plenteousness that desires to give."[186] Juliet's love partakes of this kind of "Gift-love" to a far greater degree than does Romeo. The defining character of Romeo's love is not that of giving. Instead, Romeo leaves us with the clear impression of an estranged youth, consumed with the desire to possess beauty at all costs as a way to relieve his tormented soul.

Finally, both Friar Laurence and Juliet are attentive to Christ's admonition as set forth in Matthew:

> You have heard that it was said, "Love your neighbor and hate your enemy." But I tell you: Love your enemies and pray for those who persecute you, that you may be sons of your Father in heaven. He

[181] SHAKESPEARE, *supra* note 1, at 2.2.115.
[182] SHAKESPEARE, *supra* note 1, at 2.2.132–35.
[183] SHAKESPEARE, *supra* note 1, at 2.2.148.
[184] SHAKESPEARE, *supra* note 1, at 2 Cho.1 – 14.
[185] Lewis, *supra* note 152, at 126.
[186] Lewis, *supra* note 152, at 126.

> causes his sun to rise on the evil and on the good, and sends rain on the righteous and the unrighteous.[187]

Juliet follows the admonition on the private, rather than the political, level. The friar's Christian solution is doomed to failure on the level of the city, but not necessarily on the personal level, although Juliet is aware of the great difficulty associated with loving an enemy Montague: "Prodigious birth of love it is to me / That I must love a loathed enemy."[188]

Whereas Friar Laurence seeks to impose this Christian rule of love on the city, Juliet seeks to follow the rule as a guide to her own life. Due to the circumstances confronting Romeo and Juliet, she will not live to enjoy her love. There can be little doubt, however, of the attractiveness of the lovers' decision, or the pity Shakespeare means his audience to experience when they die, concluding, in fact, that there never was "a story of more woe." In light of her faithful commitment to her Romeo—her true love—rather than to an arranged marriage, Juliet lives on as an exemplar of marital fidelity. This is a Christian message, it seems, to which Shakespeare would have his audience attend.

The families must be strong if the city is to be strong. Juliet would embrace Christian love by choosing to love Romeo for who he truly is (that "dear perfection to which he owes"), rather than according to his family name. Once she has chosen according to true love, she will bind that love in honorable Christian marriage, and will follow her love "throughout the world."[189] Moreover, she will kill herself before she will allow that holy union to be violated. It is Juliet's honorable determination to remain chaste that forces Friar Laurence to adopt the resurrection plan. The friar understands Juliet's determination and he respects it. Of course, he is also concerned with how her death may reveal his role in bringing about this situation. He seeks to employ the example of Christ's death, reproduced through Juliet, to save Juliet and to reconcile the families. However, it requires the actual, not feigned, death of Juliet to accomplish this. Juliet's self-sacrifice in the name of Christian love and marriage will prevail as the example that lives on. The problem of future Romeos has not been resolved. That resolution, it seems, requires a teaching on the proper roles of earthly and divine love. Such a teaching will help bring about a restoration of civic virtue such that the erotic, spirited youth of a future Verona may avoid the "mis-adventured" fate of Romeo.

---

[187] Matthew 5.43–45 (The New international Version).
[188] SHAKESPEARE, *supra* note 1, at 1.5.139–140.
[189] SHAKESPEARE, *supra* note 1, at 2.2.148.

Conclusion: Beyond Verona's Walls

Depending upon the interpretation provided, Christian doctrine concerning love can influence erotic love in significantly different ways. After all, erotic love can produce disastrous results apart from any specific Christian influence. Indeed, Romeo and Juliet are not the only couple whose names form the title of a Shakespearean play.[190] Antony and Cleopatra is the other such couple, and the similarities between the two couples—and more importantly—their differences, are instructive in discerning Shakespeare's teaching on divine and human love. In considering their similarities, we see that Antony and Cleopatra seek to retreat into a purely private realm of all-consuming erotic love once the republic has been replaced by the empire such that political life offers no compelling reason to remain interested in matters of a political or patriotic nature. Romeo and Juliet do the same. Both couples (although less so with Juliet) come to see their love as above the merely human, as partaking of, or approaching the sacred.[191] This, C.S. Lewis argues, is the inevitable tendency of Eros: "Of all loves he is, at his height, most god-like; therefore most prone to demand our worship. Of himself he always tends to turn 'being in love' into a sort of religion."[192] In the end, the desperation that is largely brought on by the fact that the lives they have chosen cannot be sustained drives Antony and Cleopatra to commit suicide. The fates of Romeo and Juliet are similar. These significant similarities are meant to highlight the deficiencies of a singular devotion to erotic love that has become unmoored from the broader context of life, which context requires that love be integrated with, rather than isolated from the responsibilities and purposes necessarily connected with the civic responsibilities attendant upon political life. But the broader political and religious forces that help shape the couples' ultimately disastrous decisions are quite dissimilar. These differences are at least as instructive as the similarities.

In the opening scene of Antony and Cleopatra, we encounter Antony demanding that the world acknowledge that the love he and Cleopatra share is beyond compare: "The nobleness of life / Is to do thus; when such a mutual pair / And such a twain can do't, in which I bind / On pain of

[190] There is also The History of Troilus and Cressida.
[191] WILLIAM SHAKESPEARE, *Antony and Cleopatra, in* WILLIAM SHAKESPEARE: THE COMPLETE WORKS 1.1.17; 1.3.35-37; 2.6.17 (Alfred Harbage ed., The Viking Press 1977).
[192] Lewis, *supra* note 152, at 110-111.

punishment, the world to weet / We stand up peerless."[193] The superiority of their love is far beyond what others can comprehend. Lesser forms of love are contemptible in this regard: "There's beggary in the love that can be reckoned."[194] Cleopatra is no less ready to speak of the god-like quality of their love: "Eternity was in our lips and eyes, / Bliss in our brows' bent; none our parts so poor / But was a race of heaven."[195]

Antony and Cleopatra want the world to stand back in awe and admiration of their love. In this sense their love is a means to achieve ever greater fame and glory. It is self-absorbed in the extreme. John Alvis has aptly summarized the love that Antony and Cleopatra embrace as "bidding for glory by cultivating a good consisting in nothing beyond the benefit of two, Antony and Cleopatra attempt a tour de force of self-glorification more daring than plausible."[196]

Unlike Antony and Cleopatra, Romeo and Juliet are wholly indifferent to worldly praise. Why do Romeo and Juliet not seek the kind of celebrity or public acclaim as recognition of the unique character of their love that Antony and Cleopatra find so desirable? What distinguishes the two couples? One difference immediately comes to mind: Romeo and Juliet are Christians, Antony and Cleopatra are not. Christianity's foundational teaching on humility and the sin of pride frowns upon such self-promotion, while encouraging personal devotion to God. Likewise, the first two commandments require a self-renunciation in favor of God and neighbors, rather than a self-aggrandizement. Hence, Romeo and Juliet revere love itself, but are not disposed by the influence of their faith to do so in a manner that results in a desire for public recognition and acclaim for the wondrous quality of their love. We see then in both of Shakespeare's loving couples an abstracted, other-worldly erotic love that, while assuming different forms, shares a common disdain for political worlds that offer no attractions to their souls.

Verona has achieved its "glooming peace," but what form of decent city must depend upon guilt-producing death to remind its citizens of their sinfulness as a means to suppress the more destructive human passions? Moreover, there is nothing in the uncertain peace that assures us that the underlying causes of Verona's political ills—its factional discord and

---

193 SHAKESPEARE, *supra* note 191, at1.1.36-40.
194 SHAKESPEARE, *supra* note 191, at 1.1.15.
195 SHAKESPEARE, *supra* note 191, at1.3.35-37.
196 ALVIS, *supra* note 27, at 170.

absence of civic virtue and patriotism—have been dealt with. After all, Friar Laurence and his Church remain politically authoritative in the city.

As we have seen, Friar Laurence is not without his admirable qualities, particularly in his sound instruction to Romeo regarding his unmanly and fickle "doting." However, like the Church he represents, his actions fall disproportionately short of his faith's teaching. They do so primarily because he, like Rome, distorts this teaching by using it to advance political rather than spiritual ends. In showing us both these aspects of Friar Laurence, along with the admirable example of faithful Juliet, Shakespeare clearly points us toward a political community that both rejects the use of Christian doctrine as a tool to shape and ultimately control the political landscape—whether through love and mercy or consciousness of sin—and offers a more hopeful political model. This model incorporates Christian teaching and virtues in such a way that they help shape individual souls, forming the basis for strong families that, in turn, form strong, patriotic political communities.

Weinberger argues that the problem Shakespeare exposes in this play is that of an enfeebled political order, bereft of civic virtue and patriotism. This is indeed part of the problem. However, in concluding that this problem is the result of "the extraordinary resilience and power of Christian morality," Weinberger paints with too broad a brush.[197] The issue presented by Shakespeare in Romeo and Juliet is not necessarily the problem of Christianity per se. Rather, the issue is the perversion of Christian doctrines by the Church of Rome seeking to impose the tenets of its faith on political life. Earthly love may well help form the foundation for strong families and, perhaps, open souls to a greater appreciation of divine love. Love cannot, Shakespeare shows us, supplant traditional political teaching regarding the effective means (including brute force) to control and direct the aggressive human passions such as pride, envy, avarice, and ambition. Removing the Catholic Church's debilitating influence over the political is necessary for a revival of a healthy civic order--one that can attract the interest of the city's spirited young men. Italy is unlikely to regain the grandeur, magnificence and sense of patriotic purpose that characterized republican Rome. Yet it may rediscover that healthy sense of honorable public spiritedness and respect for the rule of law if the Church abandons its extra-jurisdictional ambitions.

[197] Jerry Weinberger, Pious Princes and Red-Hot Lovers: The Politics of Shakespeare's *Romeo and Juliet,* 65 J. POL. 350, 374 (2003).

In Romeo and Juliet, Shakespeare presents to us a potential danger posed by Christianity when the proper roles of love and the law are confused. The friar would have love rule in the city, effectively supplanting traditional notions of law and justice. The result is greater death and destruction than would likely have occurred if the Prince had carried out what the law commanded, if he had heeded his own advice that "mercy murders" when it "pardon[s] those that kill." The antinomian character of the Church's teaching on love, moreover, represents another cause for concern. Romeo would have nothing other than love rule in his heart. In so doing, he becomes its slave and loses his sense of manhood. The dangerous qualities of this antinomian aspect of Christian doctrine may be endemic to the faith, or it may be a misinterpretation of Christian doctrine proper. It is the argument of this essay that Shakespeare's depiction of Juliet lends force to the latter interpretation.

Shakespeare's play about the power of love illuminates both its possibilities and its limitations. It is difficult to discover Shakespeare's ultimate attitude toward Christianity's teaching, and it is not the intent of this essay to argue that he offers the character of Juliet in order to instruct us about the superiority of Christian love. But Shakespeare does seem, at least, to offer a healthier form of that love given the fact of Christianity's having come to dominate the understanding of love in Western Civilization. In the end, Romeo and Juliet points not only to the superiority of the proper separation of church and state, but also toward the possibility of an honorable Christianity that can exist alongside and support a vibrant political community. Romeo and Juliet presents us with the spectacle of the interplay of Eros, Christian love, and political life. In so doing, Shakespeare does not provide definitive answers to the perennial tensions this interplay necessarily entails. But in revealing the failures and partial successes of the players and their fates, Shakespeare does provide the attentive reader with a rich beginning toward understanding "the true ground of all these piteous woes."[198]

---

[198] SHAKESPEARE, *supra* note 1, at 5.3.180.

THE UNITED STATES CONSTITUTIONAL HISTORY THROUGH THE BARRISTERS AND POLITICAL THEORIES OF THE MIDDLE TEMPLE INN OF COURT

PROFESSOR ALLEN SHOENBERGER[·]

The connections between members of the Middle Temple and the Constitutions and Constitutional Law of the United States are surprisingly many, albeit unknown to most American lawyers. Most recently each of the last three Chief Justices of the United States Supreme Court were admitted to membership in the Middle Temple.[1] Obviously these Chief Justices votes and leadership on the Supreme Court are important in constitutional interpretation. In the history of the drafting of the United States Constitution and several state constitutions, lawyers trained in the Middle Temple played significant roles. Five members of the Middle Temple signed the Declaration of Independence, and seven members signed the Constitution. Four signed the Articles of Confederation.

In the earliest colonial time, a figure from the Middle Temple played a major part in bringing English constitutional rights to the new world: Sir Edwin Sandys, Treasurer of the Virginia Company, lived in Virginia from 1621 to 1631. When in England he was zealous in protecting the rights of colonists against the crown, and frequently quarreled with both the Colonial Council and the Royal Governors. It was his draft of the first charter of the Virginia Company that first transplanted the rights of Englishmen to the new world. That charter provided that the colonists were to have, "all the liberties, franchises and immunities of English subjects." These included the right to trial by jury. James Beck, Solicitor General of the United States,[2] called Sandys "the father of American Constitutionalism." Sandys also drafted the second charter of the Virginia Company of 1618 that created the first legislature of the British colonies.[3]

· Professor of Law, Loyola University Chicago School of Law. B.A. Swarthmore College, J.D., Columbia University, LL.M. New York University School of Law.

[1] Chief Justices Warren Burger, William H. Rehnquist, and John Roberts.

[2] Beck served as Solicitor General during the Harding and Coolidge administrations. He was a strong proponent of American's involvement of World War I because of the moral obligations to the allied cause. He became a national celebrity in England, giving frequent speeches on the cause. The New York Times obituary for Beck declared him "one of the foremost authorities on the Constitution." http://www.moravian.edu/default.aspx?pageid=3034

[3] Lord Chief Justice Nicholas Phillips of Worth Matravers, discussed these two documents drafted by Sandys, pointing out that the 1618 document gave the first political rights to

Sandys was a leader of parliamentary thought in England. He took the position that the King's authority rested upon mutual obligations of subject and sovereign, which neither party could violate with impunity. His position was thus in stark contrast to that of King James I, who espoused the divine right of kings. Sandys was himself brought before Star Chamber but although he was bound over, nothing happened to him, probably because of his popularity with the public.

In several other ways Sandys was important. He insisted that colonists should be of high character, not felons as were shipped out to Australia centuries later. Moreover, he took the radical position (for the times) that prisoners were entitled to representation by counsel.

The Middle Temple played a role in the education of many lawyers in the American colonies. One indication of that is that 6 of 7 of the lawyers who drafted the South Carolina constitution were members of the Middle Temple. Benjamin Franklin's son, William was also a member of the Middle Temple. Although there are four Inns of Courts in London, Middle Temple, Inner Temple, Grays Inn and Lincoln's Inn, by one estimate fully 62 percent of students coming to study law from the American colonies came to the Middle Temple.

The earliest admittees from the colonies include Andrew Rutledge, from South Carolina, who was admitted to Middle Temple in 1726. It was one of his descendants (also admitted to the Middle Temple) who played a very important role in drafting the Constitution of the United States during the hot Philadelphia summer. One of the next admittees, William Drayton, became in 1789 the first federal judge in South Carolina after admission to the Middle Temple in 1750.

Virginia had the most members admitted to the Middle Temple, 46 members, including four Lees, and three Randolphs. Pennsylvania had twenty-four members of the Middle Temple. Massachusetts has far fewer, four, but of those three were from Boston. The initial patent to found the Maryland colony was given by King Charles I to George Calvert, Lord Baltimore, a Member of the Middle Temple and stockholder in the Virginia Company. Lord Baltimore died, but his son, Cecelius, the second Lord Baltimore, took up the patent and started the colony, naming it after Henrietta Maria, Charles I's wife. Because of its religious tolerance, many

---

colonists. Reflections on the Rule of Law America's 400th Anniversary at Jamestown Addresses, 43 U Rich. L. Rev. 37 (2017). Phillips points out that another member of the Middle Temple became a governor of Virginia.

Irish settlers came to Maryland, including the Dulany and Carroll families; fully 24 members of the Middle Temple came from the Maryland colony.

There were several years in the middle 1750s when there were more American and Irish students admitted to the Middle Temple, than English students!

However, several English members of the Middle Temple played significant roles in Parliament speaking out for the American colonists. Edmund Burke and John Dunning were particularly important Parliament figures. In 1775 Burke thundered against the use of force against colonists speaking on the floor of Parliament. He asserted that while force could subdue for a moment, it did not remove the necessity of subduing again and again. A nation is not governed which is perpetually to be conquered.

> The fierce spirit of liberty is stronger in the English colonies probably than in any other people of the earth {because} the people of he colonies are descendants of the Englishmen… The are therefore not only devoted to liberty, but to liberty according to English ideas and English principles.[4]

Indeed, when the first Continental Congress convened, Peyton Randolph of Virginia, a Middle Templar, was elected its first President in 1773. Randolph had gained notoriety because of his remonstrance against the proposed *Stamp Act* in 1764 and became speaker of the Virginia House of Burgesses. He was chairperson of the Committee of Correspondence between the colonies. The last President of the Continental Congress was another Middle Templar, Cyrus Griffin of Virginia. The Second Continental Congress of 1775 also elected Peyton Randolph as President, but he passed away and was succeeded by John Hancock.

A Middle Temple lawyer from Pennsylvania, John Dickenson, drafted the Declaration of the Causes and Necessities of taking up Arms, a document that rejected separate independence, but asserted that he would rather die than be enslaved. John Dickenson was one of the leading pamphleteers of the revolution, writing many missives entitled Letters from a Pennsylvania Farmer.

Five signers of the Declaration of Independence were Middle Templars. During the Revolutionary War nearly three quarters of the Middle Templars

[4] John Colyer, The American Connection, in History of the Middle Temple, ed. by Richard O. Havery, Hart Publishing, 239, 249 (2011).

in the colonies supported the revolution, but the remainder, numbering 41 loyalists had a difficult time after the war. Sixteen became political refugees in England, one died en route to exile, and another three immigrated to Canada. In total, 27 loyalists left the colonies because of the war.

During the war one Middle Templar, Col. John Laurens, (son of a President of the Continental Congress who was captured and interred in the tower of London for fifteen months) became a significant aide de camp to George Washington.[5] Laurens' language ability proved quite valuable in dealing with the new allies of the colonists, the French. Laurens negotiated the terms of surrender of Cornwallis, and was placed in charge of prisoners. He negotiated the swap of his father for Cornwallis. Unfortunately, Laurens fell to a sniper bullet only weeks before the hostilities ceased. A copy of his portrait in uniform hangs in the Middle Temple near the door to the American Library.[6]

On the British side of the war, Col. (later Sir) Banastre Tarleton, also a Middle Templar played a more nefarious role. It was he who was recently portrayed as the hated head of a troop of Dragoons in South Carolina, soldiers notorious for their brutality.[7]

Another *aide de camp* to George Washington, Joseph Reed, a Middle Templar and attorney general of Pennsylvania (1778-1780), was the target of an unsuccessful attempt at British bribery.

The Movement to a New Constitution

After several years of operation under the Articles of Confederation it became clear to many citizens of the newly independent states that the system of government was not working well. Two Middle Templars, Charles Pinckney and John Rutledge in 1786 proposed a motion in Congress for the reorganization of the government. [8] In January 1786 Virginia called for a convention in Annapolis to consider inter-state commerce. The convention was held but only nine states attended. John Dickenson (a Middle Templar) was elected to preside. Instead of deliberating substance the convention adopted a resolution asking for a constitutional conference to be convened.[9]

---

[5] Colyer, supra note 4 at 254.
[6] Id.
[7] Id. at 254-255.
[8] Colyer, supra note 4 at 256.
[9] Id at 257.

That constitutional conference opened on May 25, 1787 in Philadelphia, Pennsylvania with fifty-five delegates from twelve states (no Rhode Island representatives).[10] Half of the delegates had legal training with Middle Templars present in force.[11]

John Dickinson (a Middle Templar), it has been argued, was one of the most important speakers at the Constitutional Convention.[12] Natelson concludes his article about Dickinson:

> If James Madison was the "the father of the constitution," then John Dickinson was at least a kindly uncle. In part this conclusion can be inferred from the results, which were much closer to Dickinson's ideas that to Madison's. More importantly, we have explicit evidence that Dickinson played pivotal roles at numerous point of constitutional decision making: choosing a method of electing senators, setting the formula for apportioning the Senate, establishing the balance between state and federal powers, deciding to enumerate the powers of Congress, excluding judges from the executive veto, creating independent federal courts below the Supreme Court, protecting states from being forcibly combined with other states, and adding trust-style limitations on Congress's financial powers. One historian ... Professor M.E. Bradford [called Dickinson] "Possibly the most learned of the Framers ... undoubtedly the most undervalued and misunderstood of their notable company... He is... definitive of the moderate Federalist position of 1787-1788 and a key to the meaning of what was achieved. Professors Forrest and Ellen Shapiro McDonald agree that "the most underrated of all the Founders of this nation was John Dickinson."

A committee was appointed to draft the constitution and the Middle Templar John Rutledge of South Carolina was appointed chair of the five-person committee. [13] The first draft of the constitution was completed in ten days of intense work. The Constitutional Convention as a whole then considered the draft work and appointed a committee on Detail to finalize the draft.

---

10 Id.

11 Id.

12 Robert F. Natelson, The Constitutional Contributions of John Dickinson, 108 Penn St. L. Rev. 415 (2003).

13 Rutledge became one of the first Justices of the U.S. Supreme Court, resigning to become Chief Justice of South Carolina in 1791. He returned briefly to the U.S. Supreme Court to act as Chief Justice in 1795.

The Committee of Detail consisted of five members, four were lawyers, including John Rutledge a Middle Templar, James Wilson from Philadelphia (who had been a pupil of John Dickenson, a Middle Templar), Oliver Ellsworth and Edmund Randolph.[14] Miller notes that the Committee of Detail itself drafted the Necessary and Proper Clause of Article I, Sec. 8 of the Constitution, a phrase derived from letters of attorney in use at that time.[15]

On September 12 that committee reported and on September 15th the proposal was adopted. Thirty-nine members signed the final Constitution including seven Middle Templars.[16]

Conclusion

From the founding of the first colony in the New World to the U.S. Constitution, Middle Templars were active drafting various important constitutional documents for Americans. The rights and privileges of Englishmen were enshrined in the earliest charter of Virginia, representative democracy, the right to a jury trial and deep distrust of excesses of power by the crown or any central authority figured prominently in the spirit of the Middle Temple and its many progeny. The structure embedded in the text of the U.S. Constitution owes much to their involvement. The first Constitutional Decision of the Supreme Court, Marbury v. Madison,[17] cited only one authority, the Middle Templar Blackstone.[18] Indeed., many American Middle Templars of the pre-Revolutionary era undoubtedly met Blackstone,, Blackstone's Commentaries on English Law had as many copies sold in America as in England..[19] "Over 1000 copies of Blackstone's Commentaries were imported to America before 1772, and 1400 copies of the first American edition in 1772 were subscribed for in advance by

---

14 Miller, The Corporate law Background of the Necessary and Proper Clause, 79 Geo. Wash. L. Rev. 1, 5 (2010).

15 Id.

16 William Livingstone, John Blair, John Dickinsen, john Rutledge, Charles Coteswood Pickney, Charles Jared Ingersoll, and Charles Pickney.

17 1 Cranch (5 U.S.) 137, 163 (1803).

18 Charles Lee, former Attorney General of the United States (1795-1801) argued Marbury v. Madison on behalf of Marbury. While Lee had not been educated in the Middle Temple, he read law under Jared Ingersoll of Philadephia, who was a Middle Templar. Ingersoll himself argued Chisoholm v. Georgia, 2 U.S. 419 (1793) (result overturned by the 11th Amendment) as well as Hylton v. U.S., 3 U.S. 171 (1796) (the first U.S. Supreme Coiurt case challenging the constitutionality of an act of Congress).

19 Randy J. Holland, Anglo-American Templars: Common Law Crusaders, 8 Del. L. Rev. 137, 148 (2006).

virtually every leading member of the American legal profession."[20] The clear footprints of the Middle Temple were readily apparent throughout the new constitutional and legal system of the newly independent United States.

[20] Id.

The Attorney-General in Eighteenth-Century England

Guy Lurie[*]

The U.S. attorney-general today operates within a tension between politics and law. Scholars have already remarked that the origins of this tension lie in the English counterpart of the attorney-general in the eighteenth century. This article shows that the legal basis for the eighteenth-century tension was the distinction between the king's "body-politic" and his "natural body." On the one hand eighteenth-century English jurisprudence recognized that the attorney-general had a duty toward the abstract "crown" or the king's "body-politic." On the other hand, legal and political reality dictated an understanding that the attorney-general was also the actual king's attorney. This article relies on the diaries of one of the longest serving attorneys-general in English history, Sir Dudley Ryder (1691-1756), who served as attorney-general in the years 1737-1754, to show how personal and social commitment to the government and the attorney-general's place in the administrative hierarchy made this tension particularly acute. Ryder was well aware of his dual loyalties, and tried to balance his loyalty to the current political administration with his commitment to legal and constitutional principles.

I. Introduction

In recent decades controversies surrounding top government lawyers in general and the attorney-general in particular seem almost constant. Scholars attribute these controversies to tensions inherent in the office of the attorney-general. The attorney-general has "conflicting loyalties" between politics and law; she has dual responsibilities, both quasi-judicial and executive.[1] While one commentator has remarked that this tension began at least in the English counterpart of the attorney-general in the early eighteenth century, another has pointed to the changing nature of U.S. politics in the past few decades as responsible for increasingly drawing the

---

* Recently received a PhD from the Department of History, Georgetown University. Email: gl78@georgetown.edu. I acknowledge and thank Prof. James Oldham for his permission to use the unpublished diaries of Sir Dudley Ryder, and his gracious offer to photocopy the transcripts of the diaries that are in his possession. These diaries form the basis of this research. I also thank him for his comments on a draft. I presented this article at the fifth annual conference of the Israeli Association of History and Law, and thank the participants for their comments.

[1] NANCY V. BAKER, CONFLICTING LOYALTIES: LAW AND POLITICS IN THE ATTORNEY GENERAL'S OFFICE, 1789-1990 2-4 (1992).

attorney-general into politics and the public eye.[2] Many scholars have written on this tension, and discussed, for instance, the question of the attorney-general's client: the president, the presidency (as an institution), the public in general, and so forth.[3]

Despite significant differences between the U.S. attorney-general and the eighteenth-century English and colonial origins of this office, the legal-political tension and the question of the attorney-general's client are inherent in all offices of attorney-general of legal regimes that inherited this English institution.[4] On the one hand, the attorney-general should uphold the law without bias or favor. On the other hand, the attorney-general has a strong personal allegiance to the current government. The attorney-general of England in the eighteenth century no doubt faced the same dilemma and operated through the same tension. Or did he?[5] While the tension between law and politics existed in the eighteenth-century English office of attorney-general, it wore a different guise. Contemporaries reflected on this tension and understood it differently than our present day understanding. And yet their understanding of the tension between law and politics in the office of the attorney-general stands at the basis of our present day tension.

This article examines the eighteenth-century tension in the office of the attorney-general through the diaries of one of the longest serving attorneys-general in English history, Sir Dudley Ryder (1691-1756), who served as attorney-general in the years 1737-1754.[6] The eighteenth-century distinction

---

[2] See BAKER, *supra* note 1, at 65, and CORNELL W. CLAYTON, THE POLITICS OF JUSTICE: THE ATTORNEY GENERAL AND THE MAKING OF LEGAL POLICY (1992).

[3] See for instance: Nancy V. Baker, *The Law: Who Was John Yoo's Client? The Torture Memos and Professional Misconduct*, 40 PRESIDENTIAL STUDIES QUARTERLY 750 (2010); Nelson Lund, *The President as Client and the Ethics of the President's Lawyers*, 65 LAW & CONTEMPORARY PROBLEMS 69 (Spring 1998); Arthur Selwyn Miller, *The Attorney General as the President's Lawyer*, in THE ROLES OF THE ATTORNEY GENERAL OF THE UNITED STATES 41-70 (1968).

[4] For a recent comparative survey of the issue see: Philip C. Stenning, *Prosecutions, Politics and the Public Interest: Some Recent Developments in the United Kingdom, Canada and Elsewhere*, 55 CRIMINAL LAW QUARTERLY 449 (2010). For historical surveys of the early role of the U.S. attorney-general see, for instance: Norman W. Spaulding, *Professional Independence in the Office of the Attorney General*, 60 STANFORD LAW REVIEW 1931 (2007-2008); BAKER, *supra* note 1, at 37-66; Susan Low Bloch, *The Early Role of the Attorney General in our Constitutional Scheme: In the Beginning there was Pragmatism*, 1989 DUKE LAW JOURNAL 561.

[5] In the eighteenth century the attorney-general was invariably a man.

[6] James Oldham, *The Work of Ryder and Murray as Law Officers of the Crown* in LEGAL RECORD AND HISTORICAL REALITY: PROCEEDINGS OF THE EIGHTH BRITISH LEGAL HISTORY CONFERENCE, CARDIFF 1987 157 (ed. Thomas G. Watkin, 1989); Cf. JAMES WILLIAM

between the crown or the king's "body-politic" and the king "natural body" formed the basis of the tension inherent in the attorney-general's dual loyalties. On the one hand contemporary legal theory recognized that the attorney-general had a duty toward the crown or the king's body-politic. On the other hand, political and legal reality dictated an understanding that the attorney-general was also the king's attorney in his personal capacity. An examination of Ryder's diaries shows how personal and social commitment to the government and the attorney-general's place in the administrative hierarchy made this tension particularly acute. Ryder was well aware of this tension, and tried to balance his loyalty to the current political administration with his commitment to legal and constitutional principles.

II. The Role of the Attorney-General in the Eighteenth Century

The attorney-general was in the eighteenth century one of the three "law officers of the crown" along with the solicitor-general and the advocate-general.[7] In other words, the attorney-general was the most important legal officer in service of the crown or of the king and was essentially in charge of representing the crown in the courts.[8] Intrinsically, this office holder was placed in an ambivalent position; on the one hand playing a part in politics, and on the other hand serving lofty legal and constitutional principles.

One may describe the ambivalent position of the attorney-general in our own terms of the tension between his political allegiance and his legal duties. With regard to his conduct as prosecutor, for instance, although some attorneys-general proved to be exceptions, the attorney-general had to pursue prosecution according to principles of justice and the rule of law, and not just according to the wishes of the current king. The wishes of the king with regard to prosecutions still carried great weight, and so the principles with regard to prosecution were still shy of a fully developed rule of independence, which would wait until the end of the eighteenth century.[9] But still, even in the seventeenth century it was established that the attorney-general acts in the best interests of justice and law ("truth")

NORTON-KYSHE, THE LAW AND PRIVILEGES RELATING TO THE ATTORNEY-GENERAL AND SOLICITOR-GENERAL OF ENGLAND xi (1897).

[7] On the position until 1872 of the advocate-general as the third law officer of the crown see JOHN LL. J. EDWARDS, THE LAW OFFICERS OF THE CROWN 131 (1964).

[8] Naturally, the attorney-general had many other functions, but this was his original and primary role. For the origins of this role, see EDWARDS, *supra* note 7, at 12-31.

[9] EDWARDS, *supra* note 7, at 179. Oldham, *supra* note 6, at 165.

alongside his duty to the specific king or queen ("*pro domina veritate*").[10] This double duty sometimes necessitated balancing between remaining loyal to the king and remaining faithful to the law, especially when the king wanted unlawful prosecution.[11]

The ambivalent position of the attorney-general in the eighteenth century will become clearer if we consider the constitutional dual role that the king himself played in the terms of eighteenth-century English jurisprudence rather than our own terms. Contemporaries talked about the attorney-general sometimes as officer of the crown and sometimes as officer of the king. Rather than an unimportant semantic difference, the consequences of this distinction were important. Even the term "king" itself had an ambivalent meaning in the eighteenth century. The separation between the king and the crown or between the king's body-politic and the king's natural body was a fundamental distinction in England's constitutional order. This distinction was part of the constitutional structure of England as a limited monarchy. Jurists and political theorists defined England rather early as a limited monarchy. In the famous words of Sir John Fortescue (c. 1470), "[The king of England] rules his people with a government not only royal but also political," and thus is unable to change the laws without their consent.[12]

Jurists developed the doctrine of the limited monarchy in part through separating between the king and the crown. The idea of the "impersonal crown" as distinct from the king had deep roots in European legal history already in the eleventh century.[13] In England jurists and others connected this distinction to the separation between the king's natural body and the king's body-politic.[14] Both these doctrines have to do with the separation between the constant (the commonwealth in the middle-ages, the state in

---

[10] NORTON-KYSHE, *supra* note 6, at 18.

[11] Oldham, *supra* note 6, at 165; NORTON-KYSHE, *supra* note 6, at 27.

[12] John Fortescue, *In Praise of the Laws of England*, in ON THE LAWS AND GOVERNANCE OF ENGLAND 17 (ed. Shelley Lockwood, 1997). Yet England was not in the fifteenth century a "constitutional monarchy" in the full sense of the term, even if the king was limited by his inability to change laws or impose taxes without consent. See: J. W. McKenna, *The Myth of Parliamentary Sovereignty in Late-Medieval England*, 94 (no. 372) THE ENGLISH HISTORICAL REVIEW 481 (July, 1979) ; S. B. CHRIMES, ENGLISH CONSTITUTIONAL IDEAS IN THE FIFTEENTH CENTURY 1-65 (1966).

[13] See, for instance, Yves Sassier, *L'utilisation du concept de "Res Publica" en France du nord aux Xe, XIe et XIIe siècles*, in STRUCTURES DU POUVOIR, ROYAUTE ET RES PUBLICA (FRANCE, IXE-XIIE SIECLE) 191-217 (2004).

[14] ERNST H. KANTOROWICZ, THE KING'S TWO BODIES: A STUDY IN MEDIAEVAL POLITICAL THEOLOGY 1-4 (1957).

modern times[15]) and the ephemeral (the current government). At times these doctrines limited the power of the kings, for example, perhaps as early as the twelfth century, through the notions of inalienability crown rights and through coronation oaths.[16]

By the eighteenth century, the notion of the "crown" and the king's "body-politic" as distinct from his natural body, were fully developed. And so Sir William Blackstone argued in his Commentaries that one should not regard the king as "any other individual in the nation," lest his dignity be hurt. Rather "the law ... ascribes to the King, in his high political character, not only large powers and emoluments which form his prerogative and revenue, but likewise certain attributes of a great and transcendent nature." These attributes included sovereignty, perfection (the king can do no wrong) and perpetuity. And so, explained Blackstone of the king: "[H]is natural dissolution [death] is generally called demise; dimmissio Regis, vel coronae: an expression which signifies merely a transfer of property…when we say the demise of the crown, we mean only that in consequence of the disunion of the king's natural body from his body-politic, the kingdom is transferred or demised to his successor." Blackstone also explained how this doctrine was in harmony with the limited monarchy.[17]

Was the attorney-general an officer of the crown and the king in his body-politic, or was he simply an officer of the king in his natural body? Blackstone explained in his Commentaries, that the Attorney and Solicitor-General "answer in some measure to the advocates of the revenue, advocati fisci, among the Romans. For they must not be employed in any cause against the crown without special license."[18] The comparison to the "advocati fisci" is revealing, since the fiscus related to the king's political

---

[15] The concept of the modern state came into being between the late thirteenth century and the end of the sixteenth century. See QUENTIN SKINNER, THE FOUNDATIONS OF MODERN POLITICAL THOUGHT (1978).

[16] KANTOROWICZ, *supra* note 14, at 342-383. Through the notion of "the crown," for example, jurists developed the doctrine that disallowed the alienation of crown lands, especially in the fifteenth century after struggles between the Parliament and the kings. See B. P. WOLFFE, THE ROYAL DEMESNE IN ENGLISH HISTORY: THE CROWN ESTATE IN THE GOVERNANCE OF THE REALM FROM THE CONQUEST TO 1509 (1971).

[17] 1 WILLIAM BLACKSTONE, COMMENTARIES ON THE LAWS OF ENGLAND 234-242 (1765). I have benefited greatly from the discussion of Blackstone in KANTOROWICZ, *supra* note 14, at 4-5.

[18] 3 WILLIAM BLACKSTONE, COMMENTARIES ON THE LAWS OF ENGLAND 27 (1768).

body or to the crown.[19] And so, Blackstone for one apparently believed the attorney-general an officer of the immortal king in his body-politic.

Blackstone's views on the matter are far from surprising. In January 1769 (at almost the same time that Blackstone published the lines quoted above), as part of the case of Wilkes v. Rex,[20] the House of Lords heard the opinion of Sir John Eardley Wilmot, Lord Chief Justice of the Court of Common Pleas (in agreement with the rest of the common law judges) on the role of the solicitor-general when the office of the attorney-general was vacant. The Chief Justice argued that "information, filed by the king's solicitor general, during the vacancy of the office of the king's attorney general, is good in law."[21]

The reasoning of the Chief Justice is more important than this bottom line. His reasoning forms the clearest analytical explanation on the office of the attorney-general in the eighteenth century. He argued that "[T]he king is entrusted with the prosecution of all crimes which disturb the peace and order of society. He sustains the person of the whole community, for the resenting and punishing of all offences which affect the community." Alternating between the terms "king" and "crown" throughout his opinion, the Chief Justice obviously meant the king in his body-politic.

The Chief Justice argued that the attorney-general receives all his prosecutorial authority from the king: "The attorney general is entrusted by the king, and not by the constitution; it is the king who is entrusted by the constitution." The Chief Justice argued that the attorney-general and the solicitor-general were each a "sworn officer of the crown." As such, the office of the attorney-general, just like the crown itself, cannot be, by definition, vacant. In the words of the Chief Justice:

> When the attorney dies or is removed, must the great criminal jurisdiction of this kingdom, in his department, be suspended, till another is appointed? … Where is it to be found, that, in that interval, the noblest branch of the King's regal office becomes inactive, and the subject's right to protection is in abeyance? There is no such absurdity to be found in the law; and an hiatus in

[19] KANTOROWICZ, *supra* note 14, at 343.
[20] (1768) Wilm. 322; 97 Eng. Rep. 123. For a different treatment of this case, see EDWARDS, *supra* note 7, at 13.
[21] The chief justice acted as the "organ of the common law judges." See JOHN LORD CAMPBELL, THE LIVES OF THE CHIEF JUSTICES OF ENGLAND 296 (1849). On the Chief Justice's impartial treatment of this controversial case, see EDWARD FOSS, THE JUDGES OF ENGLAND 406 (1966).

government is so detested and abhorred, that the law says, "the King never dies," that there may never be a "cesser" of regal functions for a moment.

With his words, the Chief Justice clearly connected the office of the attorney-general to the king's body-politic – the immortal body. It is to this body that this officer of the crown owes his duty.[22]

The conclusion that the duty of the attorney-general in England was toward the crown instead of the king is strengthened by the existence of other "lawyers" in the service of the royal family, such as the queen and the prince of Wales.[23] Existence of offices such as the king's advocate-general (advisor to the king in questions of mainly international and ecclesiastical law) and the king's serjeant, point to the fact that the attorney and solicitor-general had a special commitment to the crown, not only to the king himself.

Yet the other lawyers also exacerbated the tension inherent in the attorney-general's dual duties, since all these officers were still in the service of the crown in certain cases, with the attorney-general just the most important of them.[24] Some important people in government, such as Thomas Pelham, the Duke of Newcastle, had their own "lord advocate," who had close working relations with the attorney-general.[25] These office holders had only a personal duty to their superiors. In the eyes of the government there was little difference between these officers, at least in the day to day running of

---

22 Interestingly enough, this view is comparable to the legal doctrine current across the channel, in France. There also the officers were of "the crown" rather than "the king." The English jurists were probably well aware of this French legal doctrine. See for example a French treatise from the sixteenth century that argued in this manner and was translated into English several times, including in 1689: PHILIPPE DE MORNAY AND HUBERT LANGUET, VINDICIAE CONTRA TYRANNOS (eds. A. Jouanne and others, 1979).

23 NORTON-KYSHE, *supra* note 6, at 64.

24 For an explanation of the role of the King's Advocate-General, see EDWARDS, *supra* note 7, at 131. The Advocate-General had regular working relations with the Attorney and Solicitor-General. See for example Dudley Ryder, *The Diary of Sir Dudley Ryder, Aug. 23, 1746 to Aug. 22, 1752*, entry of January 13, 1751/2, 69. For mention of the new King's Counsel, Thomas Clarke, as someone below the attorney-general in terms of "preferments of the law" see Dudley Ryder, *The Later Diaries of Sir Dudley Ryder, Selected Transcriptions*, 53. For mention of the King's Advocate-General and the King's Serjeant as beneath the Attorney and Solicitor-General, see NORTON-KYSHE, *supra* note 6, at 52. For a case debating this issue, see Attorney-General v. Lord Advocate, (1834) 2 Cl. & fin. 481; 6 Eng. Rep. 1236.

25 Dudley Ryder, *The Legal and Political Diary of Sir Dudley Ryder, 1746-1749*, entry of December 3, 1746, 1.

business, terming them all the "lawyers" and seeing their obligation as toward the current government.[26]

How could one make a clear cut separation between the duty toward the crown and the duty toward the king? If the attorney-general was the king's attorney, in charge of prosecution on behalf of the crown, could one clearly define his duties as emanating from his body-politic, rather than from his natural body? This impossible situation is the key to understanding the ambivalent position of the attorney-general. Despite the attorney-general's commitment to the crown (as a fictional construct), to the constitution and to legal principles, the attorney-general was also always the "attorney of the king." This office could not have been far removed from politics, just like it is today. The attorney-general acted daily for the current government. In other words, he was committed to the government that appointed him. Indeed, the current regime in the Georgian monarchy (the king and his ministers) and the entity of the state were hopelessly entangled in all respects.[27]

The attorney-general was immersed in political controversies. His role in Parliament exemplifies this point. Even if the duties of the attorney-general in Parliament were then less than they are today, the eighteenth century still saw a significant rise in those duties.[28] By the second or third decade of the eighteenth century, parliamentary figures recognized his role there as important.[29] As R. A. Melikan has suggested, the attorney-general had a complex set of relations with ministers and with Parliament, and was often dependent on their favors, especially since they later wanted advancement, particularly to judicial office. While they were in office, attorneys-general were political figures in Parliament, even if they also had legal duties.[30] If the attorney-general was a political figure in Parliament, how could he also serve the interest of the fictional immortal crown?

---

[26] See for example Sir Horace Walpole's letter of May 1753, in which he mentions that "The lawyers were all ordered..." 37 W. S. LEWIS ED., HORACE WALPOLE'S CORRESPONDENCE 361 (1954). See below p. 135 for the full quote.

[27] HANNA SMITH, GEORGIAN MONARCHY: POLITICS AND CULTURE, 1714-1760 161 (2006).

[28] Today the English attorney-general serves also as the attorney of the Commons. The attorney-general should thus give an unbiased opinion in Parliament when a legal question is debated including bills. In other cases she defends the government's legal position in Parliament. See: EDWARDS, *supra* note 7, at 51; JOHN LL. J. EDWARDS, THE ATTORNEY GENERAL, POLITICS AND THE PUBLIC INTEREST 218 (1984).

[29] EDWARDS, *supra* note 7, at 46-47.

[30] R. A. Melikan, *Mr Attorney General and the Politicians*, 40 THE HISTORICAL JOURNAL 41 (Mar., 1997). Cf. Oldham, *supra* note 6, at 157-173.

Another of the Wilkes Cases from 1770 brings even more confusion, and shows how contemporaries sometimes thought of the attorney-general simply as the "king's attorney." In this case, Justice Yates, when discussing the rule that the attorney-general need not pay costs in legal proceedings, since "they are considered as the king's own prosecutions," also mentioned that the attorney-general "is the officer of the king," while "the master of the crown office, [is] the officer of the public."[31]

This case was quoted by James William Norton-Kyshe to show how some confusion still reigned at the time with regard to the actual loyalty of the attorney-general.[32] I think this quote also shows that the loyalty of the attorney-general was to the king in his body-politic and not simply the general public, just as Chief Justice Wilmot meant in the earlier Wilkes case mentioned, when he argued that "for he is but an attorney, though to the King, and in no other or different relation to him than every other attorney is to his employer."[33] In other words, even if the attorney-general had a special client, i.e. the king in his body-politic, he was still someone's attorney. But in any case, both justices' sayings show the tension inherent in the office of attorney-general.

The diaries of Dudley Ryder, the attorney-general in the years 1737-1754, are a source for trying to understand the point of view of the attorney-general himself on this issue. They are especially useful, since Ryder wrote these diaries for his own remembrance and self-criticism, or at least that is what he wrote in his first entry while still a student at Middle Temple (in 1715).[34] These diaries are therefore very sincere. Dudley Ryder was placed in the problematic position of attorney-general and remained in it for seventeen years. How did he see his role? Did Ryder restrict the actions of political figures? Did this officer see himself and did he act as guardian of legal fundamental rules (the "constitution") in the face of political intrusions? Or was he more the attorney of the king's natural body?

III. Sir Dudley Ryder as Attorney-General

England saw some key changes in its state structure and public sphere during the Georgian regime. John Brewer shows how the state was

[31] Proceedings against John Wilkes (1770) 19 How. St. Tr. 1120.

[32] NORTON-KYSHE, *supra* note 6, at 75. Yet Norton-Kyshe also argued that the accepted view by the eighteenth century (as opposed to earlier) was that the attorney-general was not an officer of the king in his personal capacity but of "the nation." See ibid, at 75.

[33] Wilkes v. Rex, (1768) Wilm. 326; 97 Eng. Rep. 125.

[34] WILLIAM MATTHEWS ED., THE DIARY OF DUDLEY RYDER, 1715-1716 29 (1939).

transformed in terms of its administrative and fiscal structure. An interesting aspect of this transformation, which Brewer examines, was the commitment of the administrative class - of which Ryder was a top figure – to its pubic duties. The respect for public opinion and the fear of the public from corruption and harassment by the state were major restraints on the power of the state, while they were also a factor that allowed the state to increase its power in absolute terms, as it could more easily enlist the support of the population.[35] The central restraining role of Parliament also made it necessary for the King to rely on central parliamentary figures to promote his policies. Thus senior politicians achieved their position through control of Parliament, such as the famous towering figures of the times, Robert Walpole, Henry Pelham and Thomas Pelham, the Duke of Newcastle.[36]

The reigns of George I and George II, and especially the 1740's, were dominated by specter of the Jacobite Uprising. These uprisings were only the climaxes of a challenge by the exiled house of Stuart to the reigning family.[37] Ryder had to deal extensively with the repercussions of the 1745-6 Jacobite Uprising, as can be readily seen from almost all the entries of the Legal and Political Diary of the years 1746-1749.[38]

In a sense, the political atmosphere of the time exemplifies the basic tension that was inherent in the position of the attorney-general. On the one hand, England saw the continuing strengthening of the public sphere and public opinion, as the constitution came to limit the powers of the government vis-à-vis the English population, alongside the overall increase in the powers of government in absolute terms. On the other hand, the current regime had to deal with a real and significant challenge to its legitimacy and power, in the form of the Jacobite Uprisings. And so the government was more and more restrained by the constitution, but on the other hand it needed loyalty and commitment to the present regime. This tension is also apparent in the position of the attorney-general: commitment to the constitution and to public opinion on the one hand, and commitment to his direct superiors on the other hand.

---

[35] See for example Brewer's explanation with regard to the decision not to make use of martial law, in JOHN BREWER, THE SINEWS OF POWER: WAR AND THE ENGLISH STATE, 1688-1783 48 (1989).

[36] See SMITH, *supra* note 27, at 211 and 213.

[37] See SMITH, *supra* note 27,at 3.

[38] Ryder, *The Legal and Political Diary of Sir Dudley Ryder*, 1746-1749.

A. Ryder's Place in the Hierarchy

As already mentioned, the attorney-general was in the awkward position of being both an officer of the crown and a politician dependant on higher ranked politicians. Ryder was no exception. His biographers all agree that he spoke in Parliament, but mostly in his legal capacity, and always in support of government bills.[39] Ryder's activities support this conclusion. For example, when in May 1753 the government, and especially the Lord Chancellor Hardwicke, was trying to promote a bill against clandestine marriages,[40] the government ordered Ryder to promote the bill through the House of Commons. Horace Walpole wrote to a colleague about Ryder's exceptional loyalty in this regard, even compared to the other government lawyers in Parliament: "The lawyers were all ordered to nurse it [the bill] through our house; but, except the poor Attorney-General [Ryder], who is nurse indeed to all intents and purpose, and did amply gossip over it, not one of them said a word."[41]

Ryder himself, in an entry in his diary dated May 14, 1753, agrees with this description, and details his efforts in trying to promote the bill, without great success.[42] By May 29, he seems to have taken a back seat to the Prime Minister, Henry Pelham, and his efforts to promote this bill in the House of Commons.[43] Pelham's efforts succeeded and later in June Lord Hardwicke also managed to deflect all attacks on the bill in the House of Lords and the act passed.[44]

From Ryder's diary for the years 1746-1754, as well as from his legal and political diary for the years 1746-1749, it is clear that he often acted under direct orders from top political figures. Ryder appeared often before the Cabinet Council or the Privy Council to give various reports or to hear instructions in legal-political matters. Although not regular, these

---

39 David Lemmings, *Ryder, Sir Dudley (1691–1756)*, in OXFORD DICTIONARY OF NATIONAL BIOGRAPHY, (eds. H. C. G. Matthew and Brian Harrison, 2004); online ed., ed. Lawrence Goldman, January 2008, http://0-www.oxforddnb.com.library.lausys.georgetown.edu/view/article/24394 (accessed December 12, 2008); CAMPBELL, *supra* note 21, 239; FOSS, *supra* note 21, at 165; G. Le Grys Norgate, *Ryder, Dudley*, in DICTIONARY OF NATIONAL BIOGRAPHY 41 (ed. Sidney Lee, 1897).

40 See the background on this bill in R. B. OUTHWAITE, CLANDESTINE MARRIAGE IN ENGLAND, 1500-1850 75-81 (1995).

41 LEWIS, *supra* note 26, at 362.

42 Dudley Ryder, *The Diary of Sir Dudley Ryder, Aug. 25, 1752 to Sept. 3, 1753*, entry of May 14, 1753, 57.

43 Ibid., entry of May 29, 1753, at 58. Pelham's more prominent role after the first debate in the House of Commons is also argued in OUTHWAITE, *supra* note 40, at 81.

44 OUTHWAITE, *supra* note 40, at 84.

appearances could sometimes be quite frequent, such as appearing twice in three days, on May 25 and on May 27, 1747.[45]

In the early years at the office of attorney-general, Ryder received orders mainly from the most important minister of the time, Robert Walpole.[46] Later, after 1742, two ministers figure prominently as giving actual direct orders, the Pelham brothers: Henry Pelham, the Prime Minister (until his death in 1754) and Thomas Pelham, the Duke of Newcastle. The Duke of Newcastle was especially prominent in political cases, often giving orders to prosecute persons charged with political crimes, such as rioters in elections, or giving directions in other political matters, such as dealing with privateers who were interfering with trade with the Ottoman Empire.[47] James Oldham has demonstrated the Duke's central role in directing Ryder in context of the Vice Chancellor of Oxford case.[48] Often it was his brother, Prime Minister Pelham, giving the orders, such as with regard to rioters in Lancashire, or in the case of the Richmond Park dispute.[49] Other times it was the Chancellor passing along directions.[50] David Lemmings perhaps exaggerates somewhat when he claims that from 1744 Ryder "appears normally to have acted on the chancellor's instructions, as a loyal functionary of the government."[51] Many times, the King's hand was seen in orders given to Ryder. He either passed his orders through the Pelham brothers and the Chancellor, or gave the orders directly.[52]

---

[45] Ryder, *The Legal and Political Diary of Sir Dudley Ryder, 1746-1749*, entries of May 25 and May 27, 1747, 17.

[46] See for example Ryder's note that "I waited on Sir R. Walpole to know his pleasure about granting a noli prosequi to proceedings against an excise officer." Ryder, The Later Diaries of Sir Dudley Ryder, Selected Transcriptions, entry of November 14, 1739, 50.

[47] For prosecution orders, see Ryder, T*he Legal and Political Diary of Sir Dudley Ryder, 1746-1749*, entry of July 9, 1747, 21; Ryder, *The Diary of Sir Dudley Ryder, Aug. 25, 1752 to Sept. 3, 1753*, entry of July 7, 1753, 60. For directions with regard to privateers, see Ryder, *The Legal and Political Diary of Sir Dudley Ryder, 1746-1749*, entry July 7, 1747, 19.

[48] See the Duke's order to prosecute in ibid., entry of April 21, 1748, at 35. See Oldham's treatment of this case in Oldham, *supra* note 6, at 164-173.

[49] Ryder, *The Legal and Political Diary of Sir Dudley Ryder, 1746-1749*, entries of November 28, 1748 and December 6, 1748, 47 and 49.

[50] See for instance the Chancellor's letter "by his Majesty's command", in ibid., entry of November 29, 1748, 47.

[51] Lemmings, *supra* note 39.

[52] See Ryder, *The Legal and Political Diary of Sir Dudley Ryder, 1746-1749*, September 21, 1749, 75. Sometimes Ryder would even represent the royal family in its "private" disputes. And so, in 1752, in disputes over supply of water to Richmond Park in London and claims to open ways through the park, Ryder was deeply involved in representing Princess Amelia, daughter of George II. See for instance Ryder, *The Diary of Sir Dudley Ryder, Aug. 25, 1752 to Sept. 3, 1753*, entry of September 28, 1752, 7. But even here, Prime Minister Pelham was

Beside the clear indication of Ryder being a subject of direct political instructions, another point should be stressed. In certain cases, it appears that Ryder had little or no discretion in the matters at hand, even if they involved legal matters, such as in the Clandestine Marriages bill. Some political orders, such as orders to prosecute rioters, by either of the Pelham brothers or the King, again gave Ryder no discretion. He executed these orders to the letter.

Clearly Ryder was in a subordinate hierarchical position. The King and his ministers gave him direct orders. These orders were given in legal matters, although generally of some political interest. In these cases Ryder had no discretion in the matter. Ryder's subordinate role to the political hierarchy exacerbates the problematic position that he was in: a dual commitment to both legal principles and political interests.

B. Ryder's Social Position

Ryder was a social climber. From fairly modest social origins he came almost to the top of English society, becoming a knight and almost a noble.[53] He rose basically through merit and through a social network of patronage centered on Sir Robert Walpole. These facts influenced his aspirations and outlook toward advancement, and made him dependant on political figures.

Melikan argues that people in the position of attorney-general gained their office mainly through patronage or family connections, although sometimes merit did suffice.[54] Granted, it seems unlikely that someone completely lacking in skills could be appointed to this position. By nature it necessitated some minimum skill. But if skill was a necessary condition, it was certainly not a sufficient condition. In order to achieve such rank, either patronage, friendship or family connections were necessary. Ryder's case proves the point.

Melikan also argues, based on quantitative analysis, that those achieving the office of attorney-general in the eighteenth century reveal "diversity in their social and economic backgrounds…and uniformity in their educational experiences." She goes on to show that almost all of the office-holders (72%) studied at either Oxford or Cambridge.[55] Ryder proves to be the

involved, and eventually told Ryder not to do "anything more" about "the tithes," which were in dispute. See ibid, entry of October 8, 1752, 10.

[53] Lemmings, *supra* note 39; CAMPBELL, *supra* note 21, at 258; Norgate, *supra* note 39, at 41.

[54] Melikan, *supra* note 30, at 46.

[55] Ibid., at 42-43.

exception in Melikan's statistics. Coming from a Presbyterian family (dissenters), essentially puritans, he came from relatively low social-economic backgrounds, with family members occupying relatively low paying trades.[56] His days as a student in Middle Temple were filled with concerns over money. In two consecutive diary entries in 1715 he reported taking desperately needed money from his father, and then envying for its wealth an attorney's office he was visiting.[57] His dissenting religious background, unorthodox education, and modest financial means, all combined to make him an outsider to the regular high English society. In this sense, Ryder was a true social climber.

Ryder rose very much through his own professional excellence. He was well educated, and his diary from his days in the Middle Temple shows him reading widely in pieces from Cicero to Locke.[58] As an attorney-general he showed high professional skills. In a moment of self-assessment he wrote: "My present character in the world as to my ability is, I believe, that I am a good lawyer and [of] some parts. As to the heart, that I am thoroughly honest and of great humanity and candour."[59] On the other hand, his ability in political disputes he felt was unequal to the task. He thought that: "I am sometimes tempted to attack the enemies of the administration in a severe manner, but I check myself in that design. I am more fitted to act the part of candour, mildness, sincerity and good nature and reasoning....It will better head my infirmity and want of ability in any respect, and I think my talents are rather better adapted to it...I should therefore keep out all scrapes, all enmities."[60]

This type of assessment -- high professional ability but low political skill -- was shared by contemporaries. Horace Walpole wrote of Ryder in 1747 in a letter, that he was a better lawyer than the later Lord Mansfield, but less of a rhetorician than him: "The Solicitor-General [Murray, later Lord Mansfield]...shone extremely; the Attorney-General, who is a much greater lawyer, is cold and tedious."[61] A hundred years later, Edward Foss argued similarly about Ryder's professional merit, that "excellence of the English constitution in opening the door of honour for the entrance of merit,

---

56 For his family background, see Lemmings, *supra* note 39; CAMPBELL, *supra* note 21, at 234; FOSS, *supra* note 21, at 164; Norgate, *supra* note 39, at 40.

57 MATTHEWS, *supra* note 34, at 44.

58 Ibid.

59 Ryder, *The Later Diaries of Sir Dudley Ryder, Selected Transcriptions,* entry of August 22, 1741, 60.

60 Ibid., entry of August 22, 1741, 60. Cf. Lemmings, *supra* note 39.

61 19 W. S. LEWIS ED., HORACE WALPOLE'S CORRESPONDENCE 379-380 (1954).

without regard to pedigree, obtains another illustration in the advance of Dudley Ryder, by force of talents and industry."[62]

Sitting well with Melikan's thesis -- that attorneys-general wanted advancement to legal positions (such as the bench) rather than political positions[63] -- Ryder wanted advancement in law. This ambition probably had a lot to do with his self-assessment, quoted above, that he was unsuited to the disputes inherent in the political life. And so, in 1740, Ryder noted a conversation with the Chancellor, in which he heard mention that "all preferments of the law were first to go to me and the solicitor-general."[64] There is also evidence from Horace Walpole's letters that in 1750 there was a plan to promote Ryder to the position of chancellor.[65]

Ryder's ambitions included gaining riches and "honor." Lack of money in his early years and his outsider dissenter origins were probably substantial factors in these ambitions. Ryder was clearly very much concerned with matters of personal finance throughout his diaries. A clear example of his concern over money was his rejection of the office of master of the rolls.[66] He rejected this offer in 1738, as he would later note in his diary during a conversation with the new Master of the Rolls, due to its low salary. Apparently he asked for the salary of this office to be raised, but was refused, and so declined to accept the offer.[67]

Ryder, as a former outsider from high English society, would later in his career focus on gaining honor. He became obsessed with gaining the peerage as part of getting the office of chief justice. He mentioned in a conversation in 1754: "[M]y point now was not money but honour, that if I could have had a peerage with the Rolls as I told him now I might have had it, it would be hard to be deprived of it only because of the greater profit,

---

[62] FOSS, *supra* note 21, at 164.

[63] Melikan, *supra* note 30, at 41-69. See a slightly different position in EDWARDS, *supra* note 7, at 321.

[64] Ryder, *The Later Diaries of Sir Dudley Ryder, Selected Transcriptions,* entry of February 1739/40, 53.

[65] 20 W. S. LEWIS ED., HORACE WALPOLE'S CORRESPONDENCE 202 (1954).

[66] Melikan, *supra* note 30, at 63; Lemmings, *supra* note 39; FOSS, *supra* note 21, at 165; Norgate, *supra* note 39, at 41.

[67] Ryder, *The Later Diaries of Sir Dudley Ryder, Selected Transcriptions,* entry of December 23, 1739, 53.

and the higher dignity of [Chief Justice] made it more reasonable."[68] Ryder would hold this obsession also during his time as chief justice.[69]

Throughout Ryder's career, it is clear that merit alone did not suffice. Patronage was essential in advancement. In the 1720's, even before he became attorney-general, Ryder invested a lot of time and effort to cultivate his connections. In one month of August (in an unspecified year before he became attorney-general), Ryder spent all of the month traveling and visiting nobility and clergy around the country. On August 18 he described his dinner at the palace of the Archbishop of York. He wrote that "there were also at dinner Lord Carlisle, the Duke of Rutland, Lord Malpas, Sir Thomas Robinson and others at same table." He obviously placed more importance to the peers in the table, calling all the rest "others."[70] The two notable things he noticed from that dinner were the thanks he received from the Archbishop for "the services I did in relation to their suit with the society of Serjeants in Fleet Street" who apparently attributed the success of the suit to Ryder, and that he received an invitation to the house of Lord Carlisle.[71] All the entries from that month of August and from the next month are concerned either with such meetings or with his health problems (real or imagined). And so we see Ryder developing his connections.

Patronage was the common way to advance in politics and the state in England of the time.[72] The Diary of Samuel Pepys from the seventeenth century shows that this phenomenon was far from new.[73] Ryder himself would later become a patron for others. When he was already attorney-general, Ryder noted a conversation with a childless Lord: "He had a nephew, a gentleman just called to the bar whom he recommended to my

---

68 Dudley Ryder, *The Diary of Sir Dudley Ryder, Feb. 20, 1754 to Oct. 23, 1754,* entry of April 4, 1754, 23.

69 Ryder, *The Later Diaries of Sir Dudley Ryder, Selected Transcriptions,* entry of June 17, 1754, 96.

70 Ibid., entry of August 19 (no year stated), 12.

71 Ibid., entry of August 19 (no year stated), 12.

72 SMITH, *supra* note 27, at 213.

73 Pepys, an official in the English Navy, advanced mainly through his connections, especially his main patron and benefactor, Edward Mountagu, Earl of Sandwich, but also his later benefactor, James Stuart, the Duke of York. Pepys called Sandwich "my lord." He was his direct supervisor and Pepys spent a lot of time at his private house. Pepys' close connection with the Duke of York is again apparent through many entries of his diary, for example, in an entry from April 1, 1664, Pepys wrote: "Back to White Hall, and in the Gallery met the Duke of Yorke …; and he called me to him, and discoursed a good while with me; and after he was gone, twice or thrice staid and called me again to him, the whole length of the house: and at last talked of the Dutch; and I perceive do much wish that the Parliament will find reason to fall out with them." See SAMUEL PEPYS, THE DIARY OF SAMUEL PEPYS,(ed. Phil Gyford, 2003), http://www.pepysdiary.com, accessed Oct. 2008.

protection."[74] At another time, when Sir W. Thompson Lord of the Exchequer died, Ryder tried to help his friend, the attorney-general of Ireland, to receive the office.[75]

Ryder's first successes in advancing his legal career were probably due to the Lord Chancellor Peter King, who perhaps knew him when they were students together in Leyden, and helped many men from dissenting families.[76] They would remain friends through Ryder's career, and he is mentioned as such in Ryder's diaries at least until 1739.[77] As already mentioned, Ryder advanced to officer of the crown through the patronage of the "Prime Minister" Sir Robert Walpole.[78] A remnant of this connection remained even in the subsequent administration, as Walpole's brother Horace noted the desire to help Ryder rise to the position of chancellor.[79] Later it would be the Pelham brothers who would serve as patrons of Ryder. In a conversation with Henry Pelham in 1753, Ryder notes of Pelham: "He talked to me about public affairs with great frankness and friendliness. He told me particularly that when my son came of age he should certainly be glad to have such in Parliament as he could depend upon."[80]

The patronage of Pelham at this point served to give Ryder a strong incentive to remain loyal. His son's advancement later in life would have depended on Ryder's continuing loyalty to his strong patron and superior. Indeed Ryder himself, when considering his son's legal education, comments also on his "constitutional education":

> It is very material to form to oneself the character of the several principal persons in the Government, House of Commons and Lords, their families, connexions and interests and dependents. This will give insight into the intrigues at court and the best method of obtaining what one wants of them. Perhaps it might be worth while for me to form a plan of our present constitution, consider its weakness, either in its constitution or in the manner of executing the

[74] Ryder, *The Later Diaries of Sir Dudley Ryder, Selected Transcriptions,* entry of August 31, 1747, 67.
[75] Ibid., entry of October 11, 1739, 43-44.
[76] Lemmings, *supra* note 39; Norgate, *supra* note 39, at 40.
[77] Ryder, *The Later Diaries of Sir Dudley Ryder, Selected Transcriptions,* entry of October 18, 1739, 45.
[78] Norgate, *supra* note 39, at 41; CAMPBELL, *supra* note 21, at 235.
[79] LEWIS, *supra* note 65, at 202.
[80] Ryder, *The Diary of Sir Dudley Ryder, Aug. 25, 1752 to Sept. 3, 1753,* entry of January 25, 1734/5, 37.

> administration or in the temper and manners of the people which they must probably remedy.[81]

In this highly revealing passage, Ryder shows that he thought of politics in terms of nets of patronage ("connexions and interests and dependents") within the constitutional institutions of England.

When on March 6, 1754 Pelham died, his network of patronage, and Ryder among them, were concerned: "Our friends are in great pain lest the death of Pelham should occasion confusion. It is not clear that Pelham had quite settled his plan of elections, or if he has that he has communicated that plan to anybody."[82] Pelham's death revealed his importance to Ryder and their "friends," as head of their network of patronage. Ryder's concerns (if he had any) at his patron's death were revealed to be unfounded about a month later, with news of his promotion to become Chief Justice.[83]

Ryder's concern with social advancement, his low social origins, his network of patronage, his ambitions for advancement (both for him and his son) all came to exert a tremendous pressure to conform. Ryder's sole hope for achieving all his goals was in staying completely loyal to his political superiors. How much of a loyalty would remain to the "crown" as opposed to his political superiors (including the current king)? As already mentioned, in terms of the regular day-to-day business, especially in legal-political matters (as opposed to regular criminal and legal matters on which the King and his ministers found no interest in), Ryder was hierarchically under the direct control of political figures. He had little or no discretion. The question remains, how did Ryder act when his allegiance to the "crown" came in direct conflict with his allegiance to the current king's government? An in-depth look at cases of direct conflict between the two will help to answer this question.

C. Ryder's Attitude toward his Dual Loyalties

From one of Ryder's comments, quoted earlier, it is apparent that he was aware of the dilemma. Ryder mentioned that he was "tempted to attack the enemies of the administration in a severe manner," thus showing his commitment and tendency to appease the government and comply with its orders. But then he added that "I check myself in that design. I am more

[81] Ryder, *The Diary of Sir Dudley Ryder, Aug. 23, 1746 to Aug. 22, 1752,* entry of October 1, 1751, 29.

[82] Ryder, *The Diary of Sir Dudley Ryder, Feb. 20, 1754 to Oct. 23, 1754,* entry of March 7, 1754, 7.

[83] Ibid., entry of April 4, 1754, 23.

fitted to act the part of candour, mildness, sincerity and good nature and reasoning." And so on the one hand he felt the urge to take the side of the "administration" as its advocate, but on the other hand he felt himself better suited and perhaps committed to take the part of "good nature and reasoning" or in other words, the part of objective legal principles and the constitution. In resolving this tension, Ryder felt he had to overcome his "temptation" to be a partisan of the current government, and to at least sound objective and committed to legal principles.[84]

One such principle was the independence of the attorney-general in terms of his decision to prosecute. Political figures often directed Ryder to prosecute, and he acted on these orders showing little discretion in the matter.[85] The dilemma of whether it was legally correct or not to prosecute was explicit in the Vice-Chancellor's case. James Oldham shows how Ryder's dilemma manifested itself in the Vice-Chancellor's case. On the one hand Ryder followed government orders to prosecute. On the other hand, he thought the case should not be prosecuted, mentioned his objections, resisted and finally had some success in this matter.[86]

Lord MacLeod's case also shows pressure from political superiors to circumvent legal principles. In this case, despite some tendency to follow orders contrary to legal duties or principles, Ryder eventually convinced his superiors on the illegality of the proposed action, and together with the Solicitor-General found a way to circumvent the law. In the aftermath of the Jacobite uprising of 1745-1746, and following the capture in 1746 of the Earl of Cromartie and his son Lord MacLeod who took part in the uprising, the King set a course for finding a way to confiscate their estates while at the same time pardoning them. The Earl died, but his son Lord Macleod was potentially able by Scots law to inherit his father's estates, since it was possible for a son to do so in some cases even if the father was attainted by high treason. And so, Ryder received on January 1, 1747 a letter by the Duke of Newcastle (again, Pelham):

> [C]ommanding us from His Majesty to prepare a draft of a warrant to be signed by the King for granting a pardon to [Lord MacLeod] for high treason, of which he is indicted and pleaded guilty, in such

[84] Ryder, *The Later Diaries of Sir Dudley Ryder, Selected Transcriptions,* entry of August 22, 1741, 60.

[85] See above pp.135-137.

[86] Oldham, *supra* note 6, at 167-170. Lemmings cites this case as proof that Ryder "studied to ingratiate himself with social superiors, sometimes acting against his better judgment." See Lemmings, *supra* note 39.

> a manner that he may not be entitled thereby to take any estate that might otherwise descend to him by inheritance from his father the late [Earl of Cromartie], it being His Majesty's pleasure that he remain under an incapacity to inherit any such estate or estates in the same manner as if he were actually attainted of high treason.[87]

Ryder quickly consulted with the Solicitor-General (the future Lord Mansfield) clarifying that in Ryder's opinion such a course was legally impossible. Ryder mentioned that Lord Macleod's father had already been attainted, and a pardon of the father would not restore the son's entitlement under English Law. Ryder thought that this course was pursued because of a legal rule in Scots law that "might possibly be in view." Ryder continued to explain that "If by the Scots law an estate tail with irritant and resolutive clauses is not forfeited with respect to the issue in tail, there may be a descent to [Lord MacLeod] notwithstanding his father's attainder which cannot be prevented but by his own."[88]

The legal rule that Ryder referred to was related to a 1685 Scot statute that allowed an entail to set an arbitrary legal course of succession that was binding on third parties.[89] Ryder in his comment was referring to the irritant and resolutive clauses that were necessary to make this act binding on third parties, namely clauses that declare any deed contrary as void (irritant clause), and clauses that declare that an heir who acts against the act shall lose the right to inherit (resolutive clause).[90] The Solicitor-General answered with the proposal that was later accepted as the only way to circumvent this law, namely that Lord MacLeod sign a condition that if "any estate come by descent he will do all proper and necessary acts to convey all his estates and interest to the King."[91] However, Ryder did not think this was in line with the King's orders. He still wanted to find some way to accommodate the King's orders. But after further legal consultation,[92] Ryder and the Solicitor-General decided that "it was impossible to prepare [a pardon for Lord MacLeod] with such a condition as is proposed by attainder, as any pardon

---

87 Ryder, *The Legal and Political Diary of Sir Dudley Ryder, 1746-1749,* entry of January 1, 1746/7, 5.

88 Ibid., entry of January 2, 1746/7, 5

89 WILLIAM BELL, *DICTIONARY AND DIGEST, LAW OF SCOTLAND, WITH SHORT EXPLANATIONS OF THE MOST ORDINARY ENGLISH LAW TERMS* 800-801 (Revised by George Ross, 861).

90 Ibid., 802.

91 Ryder, *The Legal and Political Diary of Sir Dudley Ryder, 1746-1749,* entry of January 5, 1746/7, 6.

92 Ibid., entries of January 5, 6 and 8, 1746/7, 6-9.

by attainder would leave him capable of inheriting notwithstanding his own treason."[93]

This reply, attempting to uphold the legal principle in the face of political intent to circumvent it, was not the final word. The Cabinet still wanted to find a way to circumvent this legal rule and later in the year asked Ryder and other legal officers to "consider in what way the King's intent of granting a pardon to [Lord MacLeod], son of [the Earl of Cromartie], might be attained, so as that his estate might come to the crown and yet he not be attainted, whether by granting it on condition when he comes of age to grant all his rights and interests to the crown."[94] Here the Cabinet basically agreed to the idea of circumvention suggested by the Solicitor-General. It is not surprising that the warrant Ryder drafted a few months later adopted this solution, namely that Lord MacLeod received pardon on the condition that "he does in six months after he comes of age convey…all the rights he should have or has to the estate which his father [Lord] Cromartie was entitled to."[95] Basically, the Cabinet accepted Ryder's objections on account of the legal rule, and the legal officers changed the mechanism of pardoning Lord MacLeod to abide with the law.

The dual duties of the attorney-general are apparent in the MacLeod case. On the one hand, Ryder felt an obligation toward "the King's right to his interest in this estate,"[96] and tried his best to find a way to circumvent the law (shown by the lengthy discussions dedicated to this case). On the other hand, he was constrained by the letter of the law that did not allow him to comply with this interest. It is between these dual loyalties that Ryder had to navigate, in this case successfully. In final analysis, Ryder succeeded in abiding by the law while complying for the most part with the administration's will.

IV. Conclusion

On April 4, 1754, Chief Justice Lee "was struck with an apoplectic fit," and Sir Dudley Ryder was offered his office. Ryder does not reveal in his diary any great enthusiasm for this office, only anxiety over the King's reticence to grant him peerage with the office.[97] Looking back on his long years in the

[93] Ibid., entry of March 20, 1746/7, 12.
[94] Ibid., entry of May 25, 1747, 17.
[95] Ibid., entry of October 23, 1747, 24.
[96] Ibid., entry of October 23, 1747, 24.
[97] Ryder, *The Diary of Sir Dudley Ryder, Feb. 20, 1754 to Oct. 23, 1754,* entry of April 4, 1754, 23.

office of attorney-general, all Ryder could do was sigh with relief that the job was finally done: "I am in hopes I shall find the business of chief justice much easier than that of attorney-general, but must take method of doing it by general reading, by studying every question as soon as can be known before the case."[98]

Finally done with the difficult "business" of being attorney-general, Ryder looked forward to a "business" in which only legal concerns and studies would occupy him. Ryder reveals here his awareness – and weariness – of the tensions inherent in the office of attorney-general. He was certainly aware of his greater aptitude for legal reasoning, "honesty" and "candour" as he put it, rather than the partisan politics to which he was destined as attorney-general.[99] It is thus understandable that he would leave that office with a sigh of relief.

Ryder's sigh of relief must have had echoes from the throats of many of his former and future colleagues, although some probably were more prone to partisan politics than him. The tension between the positions of legal officer -- with a duty to the crown or king in his body-politic -- and that of political subordinate to the king in his personal body was inherent in the office of attorney-general in the eighteenth century.

While in theory Ryder as all other attorneys-general in this period was an officer of the crown, i.e. the attorney of the king's body-politic, legal and political realities dictated day to day loyalty to the actual king and his government. Ryder and his colleagues tried to balance the two conflicting loyalties. As the case of Ryder shows, social, institutional and political considerations pressured them to remain loyal to the current political administration. Even so, again as the case of Ryder shows, legal principles constrained them and they were committed to upholding the constitution. They had to remain loyal to the abstract crown and the law rather than to the whims of a certain king. In the face of such pressures, Sir Dudley Ryder was perhaps more successful in holding on to his principles than could have been expected.

---

[98] Ryder, *The Later Diaries of Sir Dudley Ryder, Selected Transcriptions,* entry of April 12, 1754, 85.

[99] Ryder, *The Later Diaries of Sir Dudley Ryder, Selected Transcriptions,* entry of August 22, 1741, 60.

Made in the USA
Monee, IL
08 November 2026

68032035R00049